GRAPHIC ANALYSIS
FOR EXECUTIVES

BY

WINFIELD A. SAVAGE
President, Business Research, Inc.

SECOND EDITION

NEW YORK

1926

PREFACE

The purpose of this book is to present to business executives a definite set of facts for the application of the new methods of graphic analysis to the problems involved in the management of a business.

The publishers of this book have received so many inquiries from customers as to what kind of charts to use for the specific purposes of managerial control and for analyzing their figures that the author was requested to give special attention to these points, and he has tried to cover them as specifically as possible in his book.

In order to make the book as useful as possible, a large number of charts have been prepared by the author, several of them in color, because it is felt that the superior effectiveness of the chart is just as valuable in a book as in the Directors' room of a corporation. A number of difficulties have been overcome in the preparation of these various illustrations, and the author wishes to acknowledge the co-operation of the publishers to this end.

This book is believed to be the first attempt to discuss the charting problems of a corporation's statistics from the inside, as it were. Here the attitude of the man within the corporation has been considered rather than that of the person who is looking at the corporation's statistics from an outside standpoint. The author has drawn upon his actual experience with a number of corporations, large and small, and the illustrations have been taken from actual examples rather than being made up from assumptions. The forms shown have been in successful use for a considerable time.

In this edition new material has been added on Sales Control, Advertising Control, and Production Control. The charts used are a type of progress chart by means of which close control may be attained through having constantly in view the actual performance as compared with a predetermined quota or standard.

The author wishes to acknowledge more indebtedness than can well be expressed to Mr. C. G. Bellinger for not only helpful suggestions but a great deal of constructive assistance in the preparation of this work. Grateful acknowledgments are due to Mr. G. Charter Harrison for his article quoted in Chapter VI and to Mr. Edwin A. Townley for much of the data on sales charts in Chapter III. Acknowledgments are also due to the publishers for their co-operation and many valuable suggestions in producing and editing this publication.

THE AUTHOR.

New York City,
January, 1926.

CONTENTS

PAGE

CHAPTER I—INTRODUCTION   1
Function of Graphic Charts
CONTROL BY MEANS OF VISUALIZATION   2
Common Uses of Visualization
Charts—Control Value
Uses in World War
Value in Making Decisions
Speed in Conveying Information
Educational Value
Use in Expressing Movement of Finances
Time Saving Features
Value of Continuity
Use in Comparisons
CHAPTER II—ADMINISTRATIVE CONTROL CHARTS 16
Working Capital Ratio—(Current Assets vs. Current Lia-
bilities)
Cash Position—(Cash vs. Current Liabilities)
Collection Policy—(Accounts Receivable vs. Sales)
Inventory Turnover—Finished Goods (Inventory vs. Sales)
Inventory Turnover—Raw Materials and Supplies (Inven-
tory vs. Sales)
Total Inventory Turnover—(Total Inventory vs. Sales)
Property and Plant Investment Turnover—(Property and
Plant vs. Sales)
Degree of Conservatism—(Reserves vs. Assets)
Balance Between Capital Accumulated and Capital Secured
by Loans—(Fixed Liabilities vs. Surplus)
Degree of Earning Power—(Annual Profit vs. Capitaliza-
tion)
Current Activity of Stockholders Investment—(Dividend
Requirement vs. Profits)
Disposition of Return from Operations—(Analysis of De-
ductions from Surplus)
Analysis of $1 Sales Value
Sales by Commodities or Departments
Sales and Cost of Sales
Sales and Profit
Analysis of Profit and Loss and Sales
Summary Sheet of Balance Sheet and Income Statement
Wall Charts
CHAPTER III—SALES CHARTS 65
Analysis of Individual Salesmen's Results
Analysis of Departmental Sales
Analysis of Sales by Products
Analysis of Selling Plan
Analysis of Branch Sales
Analysis of Customers
Interpretation to Salesmen
Allotment of Customers to Salesmen
Undeveloped Opportunity

PAGE

CHAPTER IV—COST CHARTS 81
   Unit Costs
   Summary of Costs
   Comparative Importance of Cost Fluctuations
   Elements of Cost—Material, Labor and Overhead
   Total Costs
   Cost per Pound
   Cost and Volume of Production
   Chronological Charts of Costs
   Analysis of Material, Labor and Overhead
   Jobbing or Wholesale Marketing Costs
   Stores Control
   Material Requirements

CHAPTER V—BUDGET CONTROL CHARTS 99
   Preparation of Estimates
   Budget of Income and Expense—12 Months
   Corporate Requirements
   Variable Expenses
   Minimum Sales Requirement
   Comparison of Actual, Estimated and Required Sales and
      Expenses
   Budget Estimate of Sales, Production and Inventory
   Coordination of Production and Sales

CHAPTER VI—ROUTINE CHARTS 117
   Use of Routine Charts in Improving and Systematizing
      Office Procedure
   Difficulties Involved in Improving Routine
   Flexible Experience of Outside Adviser
   Example of Ordering Material Routine
   Coordinating Routine Methods
   Labor Routine
   Material Routine
   Factory Order Routine
   Functional Accountability

CHAPTER VII—ORGANIZATION CHARTS 130
   Functional Subdivisions
   Interdependence of Functions
   Line or Military Type
   Line and Staff Type
   Committee Type
   Functional Type

APPENDIX A—SALES QUOTAS AND SALES CONTROL 139

APPENDIX B—ADVERTISING CONTROL 146

APPENDIX C—PRODUCTION CONTROL 148

INDEX 153

LIST OF ILLUSTRATIONS

CHART NO.   TITLE   PAGE

A   Channels of Information 4
B   Speed Test Chart 9
C   Function of Graphic Charts 11
1   Working Capital Ratio and Cash Position 19
2   Current Assets and Current Liabilities 20
3   Cash Analysis—Daily and Monthly 22
4   Collection Policy 24
5   Analysis of Inventory Values 27
6   Turnover of Inventory Investment 29
7   Turnover of Property and Plant Investment . . . 32
8   Degree of Conservatism 36
9   Dollars of Fixed Assets and Reserves 37
10   Balance Between Capital Accumulated and Capital
      Secured by Loans 39
11   Degree of Earning Power 41
12   Current Activity of Stockholders Investment . . . 43
13   Disposition of Return from Operations 45
14   Dollar Analysis of Sales 48
15   Sales of Commodities or Departments (Monthly) . . 50
16   Sales of Commodities or Departments (Cumulative) . 51
17   Sales and Cost of Sales (Monthly) 53
18   Sales and Cost of Sales (Cumulative) 54
19   Sales and Profit (Monthly) 55
20   Sales and Profit (Cumulative) 56
21   Analysis of Profit and Loss and Sales 58
22   Departmental Sales Analysis 67
23   Proportional Analysis of Branch Customers . . . 72
24   Analysis of Customers to Show Undeveloped Oppor-
      tunity 73
25   Sales by Branches and Commodities 75
26   Comparative Results Obtained by Salesmen 77
27   Analysis of Salesmen's Territory 79
28   Production and Cost of Production (Monthly) Differ-
      ence Chart 84
28A   Production and Cost of Production (Monthly) Ratio
      Chart 84
29   Cost Comparison 86
30   Analysis of Cost per Pound (Monthly) Difference Chart 90
30A   Analysis of Cost per Pound (Monthly) Ratio Chart . 90
31   Stores Control 95
31A   Chart Used to Control Purchases of Tin Plate . . . 97
32   Actual, Estimated and Required Sales—12 Months . 106
33   Minimum Sales Requirement 108
34   Comparison of Budget, Estimated Inventory and Sales
      (Monthly) 113
35   Comparison of Budget, Estimated Inventory and Sales
      (Cumulative) 114
36   Ordering Material—Original Plan 126

CHART NO.	TITLE	PAGE
37	Ordering Material—Revised Plan	124
38	Labor Routine (insert)	122
39	Material Routine (insert)	122
40	Factory Order Routine	128
41	Zones of Business Functions	131
42	Line Type of Organization	132
43	Line and Staff Type of Organization	133
44	Committee Type of Organization	135
45	Functional Organization	135
46	Administrative, Manufacturing and Selling Organization	136
1A	Sales and Advertising Chart	142
2A	Sales Control Chart	143
3A	Advertising Quota Control Chart	147
4A	Production Control Chart	149
Fig. 1	Inventory and Sales	61
Fig. 2	Sales and Cost of Sales	62
Fig. 3	Surplus Analysis	63

GRAPHIC ANALYSIS
FOR EXECUTIVES

CHAPTER I

INTRODUCTION

The real function of graphic charts is to render a service to Management. This service lies in placing before the management of a business complete information of its affairs, analyzed and interpreted so as to be readily understood, in order that this information may be used effectively in guiding and controlling the operations and transactions of the business.

Executives are appreciating to-day more and more fully the great advantages to be obtained through the use of properly prepared charts illustrating their business operations and transactions.

Such charts enable the department heads and operating men to SEE what they are doing and give them an intelligent guide and control. It is obvious that the executive who is thoroughly informed is in the best position to manage his business efficiently and profitably. Well developed graphic charts are the surest practical means for maintaining close and continuous contact with the flow of his business.

An accounting department furnishes cold figures regarding the operations of a business; various business and financial papers furnish information on business conditions of the country. It remains for the graphic chart to analyze and combine this information into comparisons of the present and the past, and in some degree to forecast the future.

1

CONTROL BY MEANS OF VISUALIZATION

In opening this chapter the author feels certain there is no exaggeration in the statement that the art of picturing or visualizing is one of the most important and effective aids that has been applied to business management.

It is necessary to keep in mind that by the terms "Graphic" and "Visualization" are meant, not merely curves or graphics to picture past results only, but graphics which will serve as a foundation for anticipating and preparing for future conditions and results. There are few phases of industry to which Visualization can not be effectively applied.

Various means have been employed in the past to correlate facts in a form which will give ready comparisons, but by far the most successful of these is graphics.

The motion-picture is probably the commonest example of widespread acceptance of, and interest in, graphics, and their development is not astonishing when we consider how clear and understandable they are.

No one can reasonably claim anything new, mysterious or untried about graphics for they are in common use every day all over the world—for example:

The face of a watch
The Sun Dial
The Gauge Glass
The Thermometer
The Yardstick
The Compass
The various types of meters

These are only a few of the graphics in everyday use with which we are all familiar, and yet, when we see them we scarcely realize their character.

Undoubtedly the use of graphics in industry came

from a realization of their value and necessity in engineering.

To-day, graphics are most effective when used to bring before executives and directors a complete, and quickly understood presentation of current happenings which will facilitate judgment about prospective decisions.

The outstanding features of graphics as a means of control are

1. Simplicity
2. Compactness and comprehensiveness
3. Vividness
4. Ease of Operation
5. Unlimited Scope

Just as money is the prime essential of Capital, and work the prime essential of Labor, so is information the prime essential of Control.

For control, these must be known:

1. What information to obtain
2. How to prove its correctness
3. How best to visualize it

Graphic charts virtually broadcast incorrectness and are the most effective means of utilizing information.

In order to appreciate the superiority of a picture over a description, we have only to look at a painting and then attempt to convey to another the impression produced on us. A description would be almost meaningless without the picture itself. Engineering has used visualization or picturing for years. No architect, engineer or contractor would think of erecting or changing the structure of a building without a drawing, nor would he attempt to convey instructions to subordinates without it. It is absolutely necessary that he have a complete picture of what is to be done.

Yet business executives often disregard this principle

and depend entirely upon memory or upon their subordinates.

A picture produces an instantaneous impression on

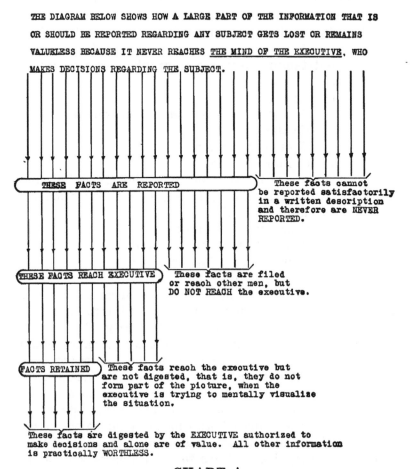

THE DIAGRAM BELOW SHOWS HOW A LARGE PART OF THE INFORMATION THAT IS
OR SHOULD BE REPORTED REGARDING ANY SUBJECT GETS LOST OR REMAINS
VALUELESS BECAUSE IT NEVER REACHES THE MIND OF THE EXECUTIVE, WHO
MAKES DECISIONS REGARDING THE SUBJECT.

THESE   FACTS   ARE   REPORTED

These facts cannot
be reported satisfactorily
in a written description
and therefore are NEVER
REPORTED.

THESE FACTS REACH EXECUTIVE

These facts are filed
or reach other men, but
DO NOT REACH the executive.

FACTS RETAINED

These facts reach the executive but
are not digested, that is, they do not
form part of the picture, when the
executive is trying to mentally visualize
the situation.

These facts are digested by the EXECUTIVE authorized to
make decisions and alone are of value. All other information
is practically WORTHLESS.

CHART A

the mind and conveys the many details at one and the
same time, with every detail in its proper place. It shows

the relation of any one object to all others so that the whole is grasped immediately, subconsciously and without effort.

This ability to present facts pictorially aids management very materially and provides the executive with modern and scientific equipment for control and supervision.

During the World War graphics were the main and fundamental mechanism through which control was secured. This included information not only of conditions at the front but also of conditions in the rear, even to the camps and factories which turned out the men and the equipment. Graphics were responsible for the small number of losses by the United States, from submarines. With them the courses of enemy submarines were quickly and accurately determined and our ships were guided accordingly. The officers spent their time studying these charts, expending their effort only in making decisions.

Visualization was imperative in war because absolute control was essential at all times. It was the first and foremost requisite of success, and this control depended on immediate decisions, based on up-to-the-minute information. The only way to make immediate and correct decisions in the face of constantly changing conditions was to VISUALIZE all the facts, and to continue visualizing them as situations changed. Decisions in war must be neither mistaken nor delayed, for not only dollars and cents, but the fate of nations, are at stake.

The executive of an army, therefore, can not afford to have a large part of his facts buried in paper documents. He must use or reject every fact reported, and to be of use they MUST be assimilated. This means that each fact must be in its right place in a mental picture at the moment of decision. Few officers in the field could build a mental picture out of these facts without the chance of omitting a great many of them, failing to consider some of the most vital points, or having the picture completely destroyed by unforeseen disturbance due to a tangent thought.

There was only one possible solution—that of visualizing these facts, not mentally, but physically, by means of graphic charts.

There is no fundamental difference between the carrying on of war and the carrying on of industry. The former is strictly "a business proposition," despite the fact that labor is not all voluntary and the element of cost is for the time being, disregarded.

The problem resolves itself into bringing together the right material and the right men at the right place and time, and is therefore basically the same as in industry. This necessitates the absolute control of activity by immediate and correct decisions, which, as we have seen, are almost wholly dependent upon the means employed to present the facts involved.

Genuine control means deciding on what you want to have happen and then so controlling conditions and factors that these things must logically take place. This can be achieved only through knowledge of facts, and these facts may be most effectively used when visualized.

Visualization increases the personal efficiency of the executive by enabling him to devote the greater part of his time to his real function of *Making Decisions*. It takes from him the laborious work of picturing mentally by having the information in the form of pictures, thus eliminating mental fatigue and releasing the "brakes" from the wheels of supervision.

We have personally had the experience of sitting with the president of a large manufacturing and selling organization who undertook to improve results by periodical visits to twenty-five branches in as many different cities, at the expense of neglecting other vital elements of executive responsibility because of the physical limitation of his ability to be in but one place at a time; and, later, seeing this same executive when furnished with a set of charts covering the operations of the business, comprehending all of the factories and branches, individually and collectively, receive these charts apathetically, but within a short time, grasp their significance and value and become so enthusiastic as to make the assertion—"With these charts I can sit in the office and run this business"—a thing which he had virtually given up as impossible.

This man had really come to the conclusion, without admitting it, that his plan of personally conducting the business was a failure, that the business was too big for one man to master, and he had discreetly assumed a passive attitude of "holding on" as the business went along of its own momentum. In a sense he was letting the business carry him along, much as a snowball rolling downhill. Few businesses can afford to carry an executive who merely "rides" and is unable to assert the kind of leadership which really leads.

As an illustration, in a small way, of the simplicity and speed of charts, before looking at the appended list of figures, take out your watch and observe the exact time, in seconds, then select from the list the highest figure and the lowest figure and at once determine from your watch how many seconds it required to "find" these figures. Time yourself in the same way for selecting the figures next highest and next lowest. Now turn to the following page where you will find these figures charted. You will see that no selection is necessary, as the principle on which the construction of charts is based places the maximum figure at the highest point and the minimum figure at the lowest point on the chart; likewise, all the other figures in ascending and descending scale. This is evidence, prima facie, that charts reduce mental effort by the orderly arrangement of facts, and thus clear the road for the brain to function more rapidly and more surely.

Production in Pounds

1921		1922	
Jan.	43,261	Jan.	43,232
Feb.	43,323	Feb.	43,231
Mar.	43,574	Mar.	43,211
Apr.	43,757	Apr.	43,212
May	43,226	May	43,221
June	43,393	June	43,324
July	43,501	July	43,875
Aug.	43,244	Aug.	43,225
Sept.	43,222	Sept.	43,224
Oct.	43,214	Oct.	43,223
Nov.	43,224	Nov.	43,222
Dec.	43,587	Dec.	43,245

Illustration has always been an important, if not the most potent, factor in acquiring education, whether elementary or advanced. Children learn first by seeing, and it is only the physical limit to which it is practicable to carry illustration that imposes a limitation on the uses of illustration as a vehicle of education either in institutions of learning or in business.

However, illustration, and the means for producing illustration has seen great development in recent years and is daily increasing in scope and adaptation. Twenty-five years ago illustrations, even in books, were rare, and in newspapers they were almost non-existent. Now, the use of illustration in newspapers has progressed to the point where we have at least one metropolitan daily newspaper founded on the principle of presenting the news of the day in picture form almost exclusively with scarcely more than captions forming the reading text.

The cartoons appearing in nearly all metropolitan

dailies are a very popular form of presentation of existing conditions, municipal, state, national, and internation-
al. Many of these cartoons tell their story with far greater force and effect than is possible in words. Similarly,

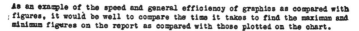

As an example of the speed and general efficiency of graphics as compared with
figures, it would be well to compare the time it takes to find the maximum and
minimum figures on the report as compared with those plotted on the chart.

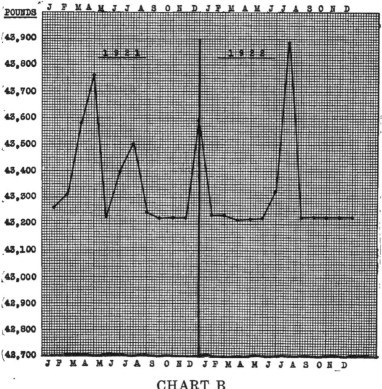

CHART B

advertising has also fallen into line in illustrating, and
not infrequently these advertising illustrations are in chart
form. It is, however, not the advertising or display aspect of charts we wish to present herein, but their prac-

tical uses and their power to illustrate business so force-fully and graphically that the observer not only reads them readily but retains what he has read almost without conscious effort.

Graphic charts bear the same relation to figures that illustrations bear to language. Each detail in the picture is in its allotted place, and in its exact relation and pro-portion to all other detail of the picture. When you tax the brain with putting a word picture together piece by piece, errors and inaccuracies creep in, both on the part of the person giving the description and on the part of those reading or hearing it; one may lean toward exag-geration in some particular, while another may err in the interpretation or in the definition of some of the words used. There is injected an element of variation which it is difficult, and one might say, impossible, to control or gauge. But, presented by pictures, all observers' minds are brought to a focus on common ground, and when the picture is discussed, one knows exactly what the other is talking of because the subject is photographed on the eye in precise shape and form.

There is a psychology about graphic presentation which is significant and which business can not afford to ignore. Through tabulation, facts are only imperfectly visualized. Relations do not stand out; they remain ab-stract. A fact is emphatic in proportion to the means by which it makes its appeal.

We may see the physical operation of a business, but to see its financial operation, particularly with a large corporation, is a much more difficult task. Physical ac-tivity of a business may be observed with the eye, because it is represented by movement of the machinery, equip-ment, raw materials and the finished product.

There is a concurrent movement of the finances of a business, yet little of this is visible to the eye. It is almost

The following diagram visualizes the results
of charting information for the executive.

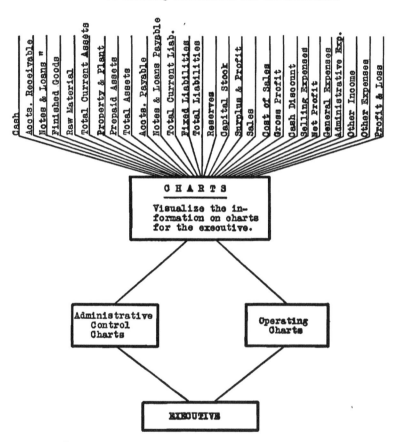

All facts reach the executive visualized on charts,
leaving little or no mental picturing.

CHART C

entirely without physical form or substance, and for that reason is harder to grasp or to control. Financial reports made up of figures require a great deal of interpretation and the comparison of many sets of figures with other related or supplementary sets of figures. The executive who is responsible for the financial results of a large business, the activities of which are scattered over a territory geographically large and possibly comprising a number of branches operating more or less independently, finds his hardest task, as a rule, in keeping in touch with the activities of the many points of operation simultaneously and continuously in a manner sufficiently informative to be of actual value in planning and directing their operation. An executive should be in possession of information which will enable him to check the accuracy of reports or statements of conditions received from subordinates, as many so-called facts which thus find their way to him prove on close analysis to be opinions instead of facts, and some of them faulty opinions. No better or more exact means seems to have been devised to effect the fullest grasp of a business than to illustrate it through the medium of graphic charts.

Details are myriad which literally force themselves on the executive to steal time needed for more important problems of administration.

Until recently, executives of large corporations found their time being consumed to so great a degree by the signing of checks that the important constructive executive work was suffering. The signing of checks is of undoubted importance yet the actual writing of a signature on a check is but a minor mechanical detail of operation. Then the invention of the multiple check-signing machine relieved this situation.

Graphic charts are now offered the executive as a similar means of relief by which to eliminate much of the waste effort and wear and tear heretofore required in the study of masses of figures set forth in reports from which deductions and conclusions must be made on which to formulate plans and policies and to reach decisions covering the conduct of a business.

Graphic charts do this because they pick up, as raw material, any or all of the figures on a report and by proper processing into graphic charts, produce a finished product of a value infinitely greater than the figures on a report, as such reports stop short of correlating the important factors. Each figure or set of figures on a report stands apart from the others, without any relation being shown on the report itself, whereas, one of the outstanding values of charts is their inherent presentation of the correlation of vital factors of a business, through the process of super-imposing one upon another. They relieve the brain of this task.

Another vital advantage of charts over reports is that there is inherent in them a continuous story of a business, produced by the very process of connecting by a line the results for each period to the results of the preceding period. Thus there is linked, one to another, each succeeding period of time which the reports of a business cover—be that period a week, a month or a year. The continuous story of business as set forth in chart form is of a value which must be experienced to be appreciated.

There arise many occasions for consulting the past records of a business, for a year, two years, or for several years back. If reports of figures only are available, each month is no doubt made up as a separate unit, and for a year, twelve such reports must be consulted and compared one by one. If there is a report available covering a year, it probably shows the twelve months of the year added together in one total, and provides no means of comparison between any two or more months of the year. Again, in many organizations, as soon as a month's reports are compiled, the first thought is "What does last month show?"; then, "The same month last year"; or, in all likelihood, "How does this compare with our largest (or smallest) month so far this year?"; and so on, ad infinitum, all with a view to comparison in order to wring from the past a prophecy of the future.

These questions summarize only the logical mental reaction of the executive charged with the responsibility of supplying the dynamic human force of a business, and he should have at hand the simplest and quickest means of arriving at answers thereto. To get these answers from reports made up of figures month by month separately entails much time and labor in getting them before him, and much more effort in extracting from them the answers to the questions that have arisen. The graphic chart, however, lays out before him each of the twelve months of a year, individually and collectively, connected and correlated so that the principle of comparative measure is inherent therein—and the measure of all things is comparative, whether business or pleasure. Nothing is either good or bad or big or little of itself alone; it is either better or worse, or larger or smaller than some other thing.

Then there is that incalculably valuable feature of charts which by reason of the scale to which they are drawn, brings out pre-eminently any departure of a business from normal, since the line or curve on a chart is thrown far out of the normal field covered by the chart if the results are abnormal, and it virtually shrieks out this fact by making the picture as grotesque as are the results of the thing depicted. Thus charts afford remarkable facility in detecting weak spots in operation and in locating errors which otherwise fail to be detected, and therefore do not receive the attention which they should receive to restore them to normal.

It is only because of abnormalities and the failure to realize expectations in business that we make up any reports or records whatever. If we knew that a business would do exactly the same thing day in and day out, and would exactly meet our expectations, it would be a waste of time to make up reports. Therefore, it being only abnormalities or errors in operating which require our attention, no argument is needed to emphasize the value of the principle in charts which makes the vital points requiring attention fairly stand up and shout for that attention, while the normal or expected things recede into the background and gracefully eliminate themselves as if recognizing that they have no valid or justifiable claim on the time of the executive.

Elements which enter into the study of stabilization of profits must be visualized in order to bring forth the irregularities that characterize the average business.

The subsequent charts in this book elucidate a principle for the interpretation of business facts which is without equal.

CHAPTER II

ADMINISTRATIVE CONTROL CHARTS

Administrative Control charts provide means by which the business executive, laying no claim to expert financial training, may read from his Balance Sheet and Income Statement more vital facts of his business than he has customarily been able to find in his reports.

They enable him to grasp conditions immediately and comprehensively, and without great mental effort, as they visualize in definite form the activities and trends of the various phases of the business. The contents of a Balance Sheet or Income Statement may be interesting in themselves but mean little until relationships are completed and portrayed.

The amounts of inventory, plant investment, or current liabilities as shown on the ordinary balance sheet, express a monetary value, but their real value is fully understood only when their relation to capital is measured together with the turnover of inventories, the turnover of plant investment, and the ratio of current assets to current liabilities read by means of relationships.

The financial and operating statistics of a business contain the most intimately related facts, and their greatest value lies in the establishment of these relationships. By them a complete analysis is developed, which gives thorough knowledge for directing and controlling the operation of a business.

16

A comprehensive set of charts which will bring all of the administrative factors of a business directly under the eye in a form which will prove most valuable has long been in demand by the busy executive.

Such a set is shown herein and was especially designed to facilitate administrative control.   .

A list of the contents and purposes of these charts follows:

Relation of Current Assets to Current Liabilities shows—Degree of
       liquidity and working capital ratio.
" " Cash to Current Liabilities shows—Cash Position.
" " Accts. Receivable to Sales shows—The Collection Policy.
" " Sales to Finished Goods shows—Finished Goods Inven-
       tory Turnover.
" " Sales to Materials and Supplies shows—Condition of
       Inventory.
" " Sales to Total Inventory shows — Total Inventory
       Investment Turnover.
" " Sales to Property and Plant shows—Turnover of Plant
       Investment.
" " Reserves to Total Assets shows—Degree of Conservatism.
" " Fixed Liabilities to Surplus shows—Balance between
       capital accumulated and capital secured by loans.
" " Profit & Loss to Capitalization shows—Degree of earning
       power.
" " Surplus for the period (after dividend on
    1st preferred stock), to Common Dividend
    requirements shows — Current activity of stockholders'
       investment.

Analysis of Surplus   shows The ultimate advantage
           to which the business has
           operated.

Analysis of $1 Sales Value " What constitutes a $1
           Sales Value.

Sales by Commodities " Comparative Sales by
           months and cumulatively.

Sales and Cost of Sales " Periodic Sales, Cost .&
           relative values.

Profit and Sales   " The periodic Sales and
           profit.

Analysis of Profit & Sales " The proportional value of
           net operating Profit and
           Sales annually.

Summary Sheet   " Analyses of the facts vis-
          ualized on the charts.

Desirable limits must be established for each of the factors named, but it should be borne in mind that these vary according to the kind of business and should not be determined arbitrarily. Where the budget system is used, the budget estimate will in some degree serve as a guide.

Degree of Liquidity and Working Capital Ratio— T h e working capital ratio, or relation of current assets to current liabilities, is probably the most commonly known measure applied to financial statements and is most frequently noted in studying a business with a view to extending credit. The maintenance of adequate working capital in a business and a good working capital ratio are of the greatest importance. Lack of sufficient working capital might hinder operations and create an unfavorable credit position. The ratio indicates the ability to liquidate under pressure of a crisis.

It is important to know exactly this relationship but the mind should not be burdened with retaining these figures from month to month. A chart will show these relationships monthly for an indefinite period, while without such a chart additional mental effort is necessary to get the true value of these elements. A chart shows precisely what the condition is at the close of any period, thereby converting these items on the balance sheet from mere figures to business facts from which deductions as to future conditions may readily be made. The value of this chart, like that of all charts, is cumulative.

This particular chart, No. 2, for example, shows that the current liabilities between January and October, 1921, increased in approximately the same amount ($70,000 and $65,000 respectively). If presented by figures alone, they would tend to convey the impression that this would constitute no marked change in the condition of the business. Chart No. 1 shows clearly, however, that the increases, though in approximately the same amounts, were by no means in the same proportion, and that, while in January 1921 there were $8.90 of current assets to every dollar of current liabilities, in October there were but $2.70 of cur-

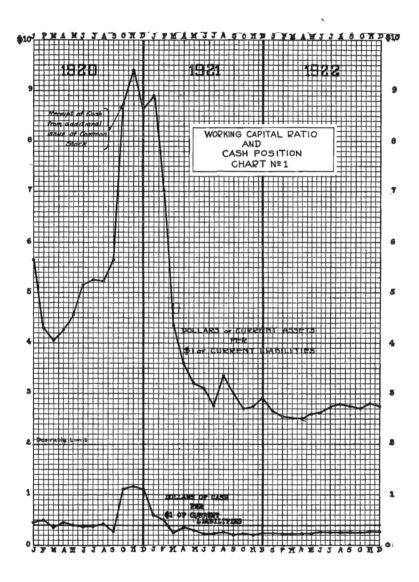

WORKING CAPITAL RATIO
AND
CASH POSITION
CHART №1

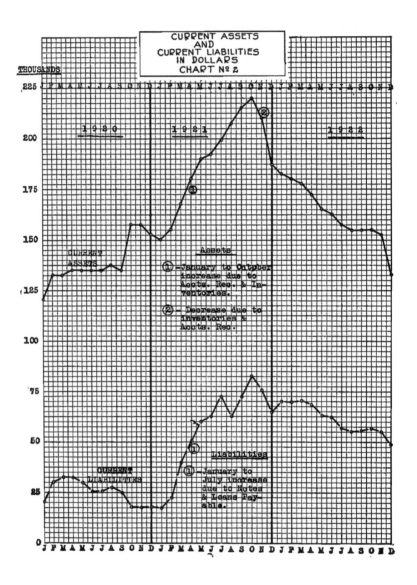

rent assets to every dollar of current liabilities.

It also clearly shows that expansion of current assets and current liabilities as shown in 1921 on chart No. 2 on the same capital, means a lower ratio of current assets to current liabilities and inversely on contraction of these elements.

Figures alone are apt to be deceiving and only a considerable training in accounting and finance will enable one to analyze fully the significance of what has taken place during a period, while charts reflect this automatically and instantaneously and may be likened to a signal system on a railroad.

Cash Position—It is seen on Chart No. 1 that cash played no important part in the proportional variation of current assets and current liabilities until October, 1920 and then only as a result of the receipts from an additional issue of common stock. Ordinarily, cash, as reflected on the chart is not sufficient to vary the trend of the curve showing $1 of current assets per $1 of current liabilities, but nevertheless it is one of the most important of the current assets.

Cash was included on Chart No. 1 because it is the most active of the current assets and should be measured with and by current liabilities. The monetary value represented by cash is not really appreciated until consideration is given the current liabilities which must be liquidated with cash.

In this instance the desirable limit was 40 cents of cash per $1 of current liabilities. In other words, it was considered unfavorable if the current liabilities were more than 2½ times the cash on hand.

As a result of the increase in Current Liabilities between March 1921 and December 1922 shown on Chart No. 2, the cash on hand represented a smaller proportion than the limit established during this period.

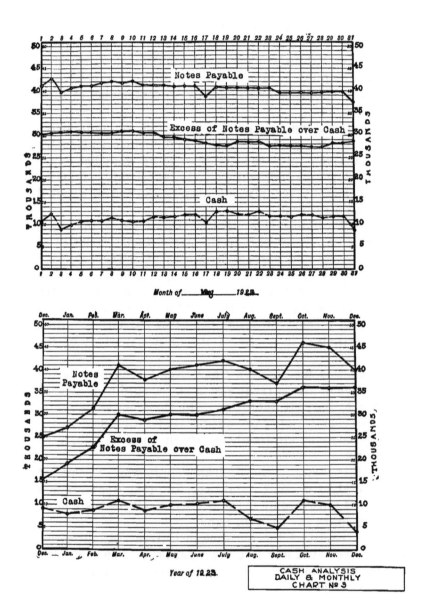

Month of ____ May ____ 19 23.

Year of 19. 23.

CASH ANALYSIS
DAILY & MONTHLY
CHART № 3

Another analysis of the cash situation is shown on Chart No. 3 where notes payable, cash and the net balance are shown both daily and monthly. Sufficient supply of cash is the first requisite of a business, and such charts will show exactly the relative value of cash and its relation to current liabilities. They enable the executive, and particularly the Treasurer, to keep before him continuously exactly what his cash is in dollars as compared with outstanding current notes payable and the excess of notes payable over cash.

The upper black line represents the Notes Payable in Dollars, the middle black line represents Excess of Notes Payable over cash, and the broken black line represents cash in hand.

If every dollar of cash in hand were used to liquidate the outstanding notes payable, the balance still unpaid would be represented by the middle line.

Collection Policy—Accounts Receivable virtually represent the uncollected sales values the customer is using without any assessment and which are frequently replaced by borrowed capital for which interest is paid, thereby reducing the margin of profit from these sales.

Therefore they become a very important factor which should be constantly under observation.

Accounts Receivable analysis gives the collection manager a close and intelligent knowledge of his accounts, but it is by no means the kind of detail to be submitted to the executive. It is sufficient for the executive to know what the collection policy is, and if results are unsatisfactory an explanation may be obtained from the credit manager.

The turnover of accounts receivable is most effectively stated in the number of average days' sales represented in outstanding accounts receivable. An increase in the turnover of accounts receivable results in added net profits on the original investment.

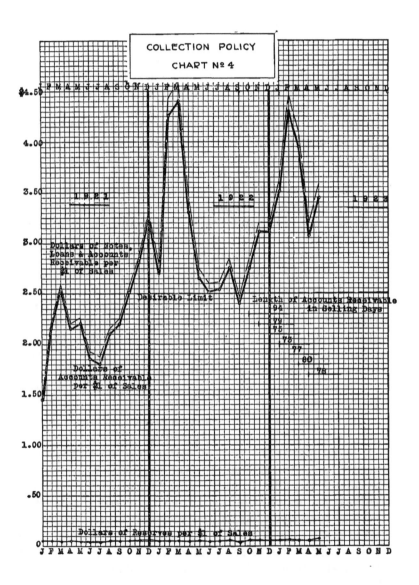

Since Accounts Receivable are a direct result of sales it is necessary that they be measured by them, and in order to show their true condition to the executive clearly and concisely they must be presented in a simplified form.

For the purpose of illustration, there are included on Chart No. 4 the notes and loans receivable. These notes and loans represent old accounts receivable for which notes have been given and a small amount of loans made to some of these customers in order to help them over a difficult period.

They originated several years back and have been carried ever since and really should have been written off as Bad Debts. But for the purpose of making a good financial showing they were included.

However, when the executive saw his accounts receivable visualized he immediately investigated and had them written off 50%.

Another interesting revelation was that the Reserve for Bad Debts was set up at 5 cents on every dollar of sales regardless of the age of the Accounts Receivable.

The last year on Chart No. 4 shows that accounts receivable have not once been less than $3 to $1 of sales. This means that for $3 of sales the best that could be done was to collect $1 within the credit period allowed, and in one instance, February, there was $4.25 outstanding for every $1 of sales.

Converting these figures into selling days shows that they have ranged from 78 to 94 days; or in other words, sales made in April would not be paid for until the middle of July at the current rate of collections.

For the purpose of overcoming mental effort and endless detail, Chart No. 4 was constructed. It shows the proportion of sales uncollected, the length of accounts receivable in selling days, the proportion of old accounts that have been converted into notes and loans, as well as the proportion set aside as bad debts, uncollectible; thus giving a complete history of the accounts receivable in a simple and complete form.

This chart enables the executive with his knowledge of the business to forecast probable collections with considerable accuracy; it shows the sales and collections and automatically sets the pace for the latter.

Finished Goods and Total Inventory Turnover and Condition of Material and Supplies Inventory— During the fiscal year or any given period of a business, two things are disposed of or turned over:

1. Stock of materials.
2. Money invested in inventory.

The rate at which these two elements move has a very definite effect on the profits; and an efficient control will go far toward securing maximum profits with a given capital, or a given profit with a minimum capital.

No matter how fast goods move or how rapidly the investment in finished goods is replaced, if an elaborate investment is required in order to produce the stock or merchandise investment, the turnover of capital necessary to replace it would be slow and the business might be made more successful from the standpoint of profits.

In the final analysis the turnover is not an end in itself but merely a means to an end, namely, net profit, for the more rapidly the investment in inventories is turned over, the smaller the amount of capital required to finance a given volume of business.

Since inventories are created to meet sales it is only logical that they should be measured by them.

On Chart No. 5 are shown the values of Raw Materials and Supplies, Finished Goods and Total Inventories as compared with Sales in dollar values. It shows immediately the Inventories representing SUPPLY, as compared with sales representing DEMAND.

The money tied up in excess inventory may be readily compared with that of Accounts Receivable, for each represents "Current Assets" which are not "working" and which may depreciate through market depression or busi-

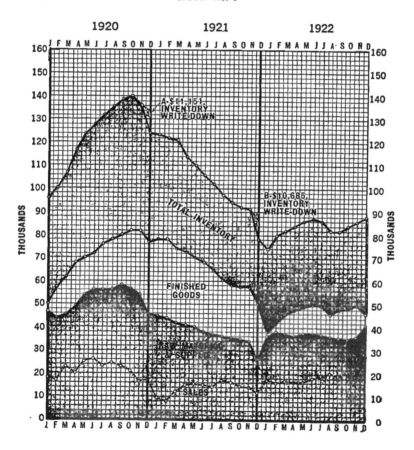

ANALYSIS OF INVENTORY VALUES
INTO
FINISHED GOODS & RAW
MATERIALS & SUPPLIES
CHART No. 5

ness failures.

A case that came under personal observation was one where a large corporation, using tin-plate in turning out its product was carrying a stock of that material amounting to $300,000 as against a monthly consumption amounting to $20,000. By throwing the chart light on this particular spot, it was possible to reduce their average stock of tin-plate to about $75,000, thus releasing more than $200,000 of cash, which they could, of course, use to marked advantage. Details of the manner in which this was accomplished are set forth in a later chapter.

No executive is capable of memorizing or co-ordinating the figures shown on the many reports he receives and it is the attempt to mentally visualize their relative values that consumes much of his time.

With these charts he has material for immediate judgment and decision.

The desirable limit of $0.50 of sales each month for every dollar of finished goods shown on Chart No. 6, if maintained would give an approximate turnover six times annually, of each month's finished goods. Of course, there is a margin of profit in sales but the above is sufficiently accurate for the executive to show him the rate at which the inventory is moving.

It also shows whether the demand warrants the existing inventory of raw materials and supplies.

Some measurement by which inventories may be controlled is desirable and to that end these charts were developed.

Chart No. 6 shows these same values in business language, that is, on a dollar basis, at the same time automatically giving percentages, since 100 cents equals a dollar as well as 100 per cent in this instance. In this way the excess inventory carried month by month is instantaneously shown as well as an accurate idea of the excess

money tied up.
    Figures shown on Chart No. 6 in October, 1921, indi-
cate 24 cents (Fig. "1") of sales for every dollar of finished goods inventory, 41 cents (Fig. "2") of sales per one
dollar of raw material and supplies inventory, and 15½

TURNOVER OF FINISHED GOODS
INVENTORY & CONDITION OF
RAW MATERIALS & SUPPLIES INVENTORY
CHART No. 6

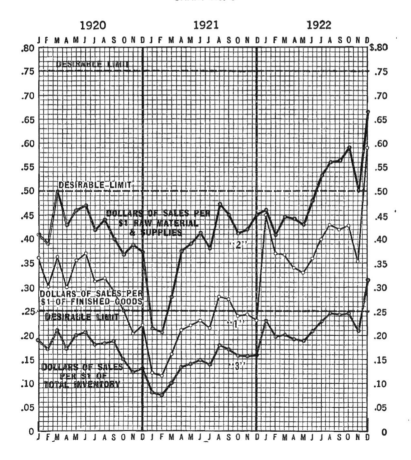

cents (Fig. "3") of sales for every dollar of total inventory (figures being: sales $14,000, finished goods $58,000, and total inventory $92,000); 76 cents is tied up in finished goods, or a sufficient supply to last approximately four months. The sales for the month of October represent 15½ per cent of the total investment in inventory and if no further purchases were made, production could continue for approximately 6½ months before the total inventory would be exhausted. This shows a turnover of the October inventory of only twice a year, whereas the desirable limit calls for a turnover six times a year. This condition showed steady improvement as portrayed by the total inventory line (green) which gradually approached the "desirable limit" line in January, 1922. In December it finally intersected and crossed the "desirable limit" line, showing a greatly improved condition. This illustrates how the establishment of the relation of two factors of a business, by means of properly locating them on a chart, sets forth clearly and simply the position of important elements of a business, showing their trend and whether they are becoming more favorable or less favorable.

It will be noted how simple it is to establish, mathematically, a desirable limit, by the mere operation of drawing what may be termed a "desirable limit" line horizontally across the chart at the point determined upon, so that wherever its complementary line intersects this "desirable limit" line, it constitutes a warning which is set up right in the path of the observer, so that no mental effort is necessary to perceive the warning.

Turnover of Property and Plant Investment— The proportionate value of Sales to property and plant investment expresses the relationship of the volume of business to the capital invested in property and plant.

In most instances a large majority of Fixed Assets

represent means of production and are therefore directly related to Sales. This relation measures the economic necessity of the assets.

Monetary values of property and plant carried on the books represent their established value, whether derived from periodic depreciation applied to them or from appraisals, or both; and they mean very little outside of the investment represented, unless other factors are taken into consideration. The average investor would not buy securities that yielded only 2 or 3 per cent annually, yet many will become financially interested in a corporation without giving full consideration to the earning power shown. Unless the net return is greater than that yielded by gilt-edged securities, the venture may be classed as a failure, considering the worry and effort on the part of the investors and administrators.

By measuring property and plant investment by sales, consideration is given the value of these investments, as over-valuation is reflected in costs and is a financial burden.

A conservative investment in property and plant is a decided advantage in meeting competition.

Excessive investment in property and plant creates a burden of overhead expense which is a permanent competitive disadvantage to a business. Such a situation is remedied by

    1. Reduction of property and plant
    2. Increased volume of business.

The desirable limit of 18 cents of sales each month for each dollar of property and plant invested, shown on Chart No. 7, gives a turnover of 2.16 times annually. This may seem high but a high rate of turnover should be maintained.

Chart No. 7 exhibits this ratio of sales to property and plant investment by line "A"—"B", showing but

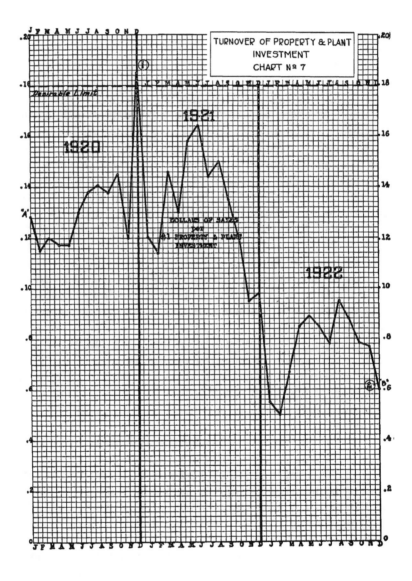

TURNOVER OF PROPERTY & PLANT
INVESTMENT
CHART N⁰ 7

12.8¢ sales in January, 1920, to $1 of Property & Plant investment rising to 18.5¢ (1) in December, 1920, and dropping to 6¢ (2) in December, 1922, for every dollar of Property & Plant investment.

The establishing of the straight line fixing a desirable limit gives a standard to work to, fixing it not only on paper, but in the mind also, and applying it each month in a way that might be termed automatic.

The rate of turnover set as a desirable limit for any one period must not be adopted as a standard for all times. Competitive conditions, the character of the business and properties required in the conduct of the business in any industry should regulate the rate of turnover.

It seems incredible that the annual profit of a business should represent as little as 6 cents on every dollar invested in property and plant, yet as a result of over-expansion, many large corporations are carrying as assets fixed investments that are more in the nature of liabilities.

Chart No. 7 will bring home the necessity for proper consideration of property and plant investment and the importance of visualizing its proportionate value to sales.

As an example let us consider the month of November, 1922 when the sales represented 7.7 cents for every dollar of property and plant. The balance sheet showed property and plant values to be $184,405, and the income statement showed that sales were $14,150 for the month, and net profit $866.

Considering the two items of $184,405 and $14,150 there seems to be no significant relation between them, yet when their proportional value is shown, it immediately means something.

A further analysis shows:

Property and Plant, Nov., 1922....$184,405
Sales, Nov., 1922 14,150
Dollars of sales per $1 of property
    and plant .... $ .0770
Dollars of Net profit for the month
    per $1 of property and plant.. .0046

At the rate of $.0046 dollars return monthly in net profit for every dollar invested in property and plant it would take approximately 20 years to replace the investment, disregarding the necessary appropriation of profits for dividends, etc.

The month selected (November, 1922) represented the average net profit for the twelve months, and by multiplying $ .0046 by twelve we get $ .0552 return annually on each dollar invested in property and plant. This represents only 5.52% return annually. Many securities could be bought in the open market that would yield a greater return than 5.5%.

Chart No. 7 gives an instantaneous and invaluable interpretation of the figures shown on the balance sheet and income statement in a way that induces more accurate conclusions and management. An executive need only investigate when the proportion is below the desirable limit, when he realizes that the excess of property and plant investment is eating up the earnings and jeopardizing future profits.

The executive does not have to wait for the auditor's report to know that the sales are not keeping pace with the plant investment. He quickly realizes the situation when the curve continues below the desirable limit.

Degree of Conservatism—The most common forms of reserves are those established for depreciation and bad debts and since they are established out of the profits accruing, it is necessary that the degree to which these reserves are being established be known, not only in dollars and cents but in such a way that their effect on profit and loss may be readily determined.

Excessive reserves will result in the showing of unduly reduced earnings and unnecessarily high costs, since these reserves must be charged into operating costs.

On Charts Nos. 8 & 9 only profit and loss reserves have been taken into consideration as these are what we call essential reserves, inasmuch as they are necessary to determine the actual net profit.

Besides the above mentioned profit and loss reserves there are various classes of surplus reserves and reserves for unforeseen expenses but since they are more or less nominal and varied no mention is made of them.

Chart No. 8 shows the RATE of variation of the reserves and indicates that the amounts set aside as reserves during 1921 and 1922 were considerably less in proportion than in 1920, the variation being between 8 and 9 cents in 1920 and between 5 and 6 cents in 1922.

The semi-logarithmic (or ratio) paper used for this chart permits the graphic presentation of changes in every quantity on the same basis without respect to the magnitude of the quantity itself.

This type of chart shows variations in relative value of each factor without necessarily referring to the quantity and in doing so brings out the RATE of change taking place.

For some purposes a ratio (or semi-logarithmic) chart has an advantage over the difference chart, where ratios of growth or reduction are desired. A consistently straight line on a ratio chart means uniformity in percentage growth, while the same uniformity of growth on a difference chart will be represented by a line which will not run straight but will change direction.

Where forecasts are made by assuming a certain rate

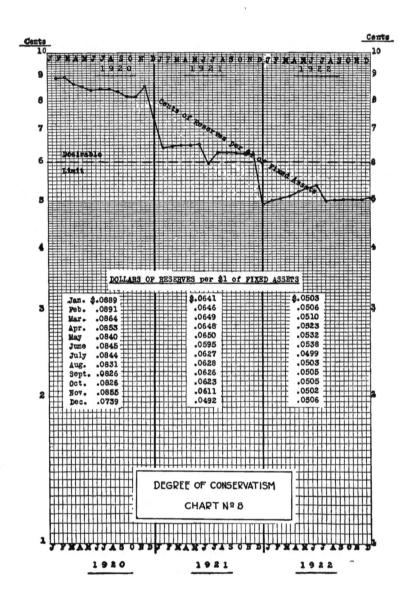

DOLLARS OF RESERVES per $1 of FIXED ASSETS

Jan. $.0889	$.0641	$.0503
Feb. .0891	.0646	.0506
Mar. .0864	.0649	.0510
Apr. .0853	.0648	.0523
May .0840	.0650	.0532
June .0845	.0595	.0538
July .0844	.0627	.0499
Aug. .0831	.0628	.0503
Sept. .0826	.0626	.0505
Oct. .0826	.0623	.0505
Nov. .0855	.0611	.0502
Dec. .0739	.0492	.0506

DEGREE OF CONSERVATISM

CHART Nº 8

1920   1921   1922

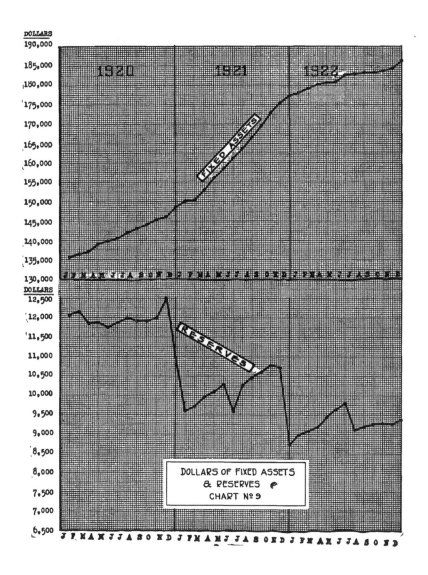

DOLLARS OF FIXED ASSETS
& RESERVES
CHART № 9

of growth, ratio charts are advantageous, since a forecast is made by simply drawing a straight line or extending a line already drawn to represent the rate experienced in the past. Equal rates of growth are clearly shown by parallel lines. See Haskell's, "Graphic Charts in Business," page 50.

Thus logarithmic charts are used to exhibit comparisons on a percentage basis and not to show actual differences between two or more factors. Logarithmic charts show percentage difference clearly for the reason that equal changes in percentage of two or more factors charted will cause the lines on the chart to run exactly parallel, and they will deviate from parallel in proportion to the deviation in percentage.

Balance Between Capital Accumulated and Capital Secured by Loans— Business corporations separate Capital and Profits by calling the latter Surplus, which represents the accumulation of profits from operations.

This surplus represents the profits accruing to the credit of the owners or stockholders, and when compared with liabilities shows the relation between this amount accumulated by operations and the money interest of creditors or amount secured by loans.

The ratio or percentage of Fixed Liabilities to Surplus and Profits is shown on Chart No. 10.

A high ratio means proportionately heavy fixed liabilities and in such cases reduction in earnings will seriously threaten the business. On the other hand, if the business goes well and the borrowed capital is used profitably, this ratio will be reduced.

Bondholders are especially interested in seeing a low ratio of Liabilities to Surplus because the latter represents the claim supporting their loans.

Since the dividends to holders of common stock are limited in amount only by the profits it is natural that

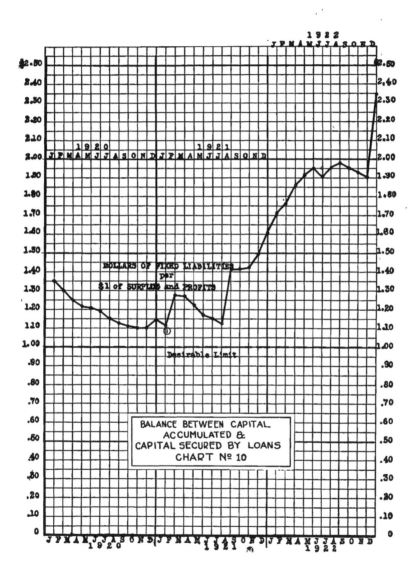

BALANCE BETWEEN CAPITAL
ACCUMULATED &
CAPITAL SECURED BY LOANS
CHART Nº 10

these stockholders should also have a vital interest in this ratio.

Chart No. 10 indicates that business expansion was built up on borrowed rather than owned capital.

There is a risk attached to the condition where borrowed exceeds owned capital, when creditors press for payment.

This chart shows that the fixed liabilities, to each $1.00 of surplus, climbed steadily from $1.10 in February, 1921 ("1") to $2.35 in December, 1922, showing an adverse trend, as this proportionate increase of fixed liabilities is almost uninterrupted during this period of two years, and at the end of that period had reached more than double the desirable limit as set by the horizontal line across the chart at the $1.00 mark on the scale.

It is no part of the purpose of this book or of any chart to exhibit or emphasize the unfavorable aspect of things, but merely to present facts unbiased.

Degree of Earning Power—The degree of economy and efficiency in the use of capital in a business is measured by the turnover of the total capital used. The turnover of capital is a general measure, as it includes and summarizes the turnover of inventories, accounts receivable and plant investment. By visualizing this turnover the broad trends in a business and the cause for unfavorable results may be determined and specifically pointed out by analysis of the supporting turnovers.

Chart No. 11 shows the annual capital and the net return for a period of fourteen years. The curve shows the annual trend and the small diagonal-lined blocks show what proportion of the total investment the profit represented. The turnover of capital is automatically determined by the figure representing the annual return per one dollar of capital stock.

It may also be observed that when additional stock

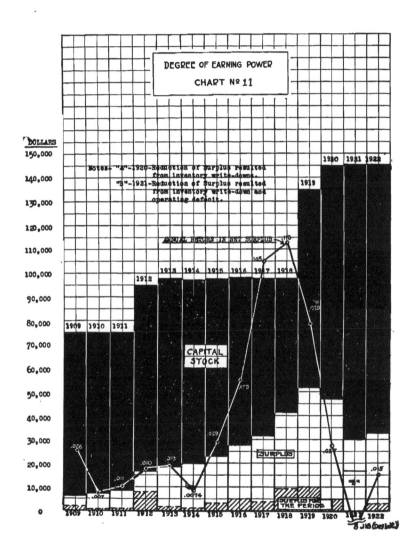

was issued in 1919 and 1920, the net proportional return decreased, especially in 1921 when a loss of 11.8 cents on every dollar of capital stock was incurred, as exhibited by the curve which shows the annual profit or surplus earned on each dollar of capital stock.

This chart shows the value (at par) of the capital stock outstanding, and increases in the capital stock from time to time, this being exhibited by the increasing height of the black columns. These increases in capital stock starting with $75,000 in 1909, were as follows:

> 1912 increase $20,000 to $95,000
> 1913   "   3,000 "   98,000
> 1919   "   37,000 " 135,000
> 1920   "   10,000 " 145,000

The net profit or surplus for each year is represented by the extreme bottom portion of each of the white blocks. This surplus, starting with $7,000 in 1909, accumulates each year until it reaches $52,000 in 1919. It then decreases until 1921, when it recedes to $30,000 and in 1922 it again rises to $33,000.

Current Activity of Stockholders' Investment—Dividends are declared and paid from the earnings of a company, and only by measuring the dividend requirements by the earnings each month is the Executive in a position to see exactly to what ultimate advantage his organization is operating.

Chart No. 12 shows exactly each month what is left for the common stockholders after consideration is given the preferred stockholders.

On this chart, No. 12, the dividend is not being earned unless the "Profit" line (solid black) runs up more sharply than the "Common Dividend Requirement" line (dotted black); thus in 1920, when the common dividend required $6,500, the actual earnings (solid black line) were $12,750. In 1921, with common dividend requirements the same,

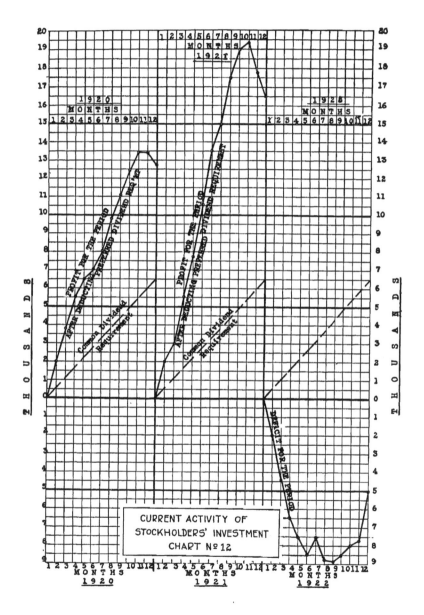

CURRENT ACTIVITY OF
STOCKHOLDERS' INVESTMENT
CHART № 12

earnings were $16,500, but in 1922, with common dividend requirements still the same, there was no profit made but a loss of $5,000 was sustained, as shown by the line "Deficit for the Period" (solid black).

Disposition of Return from Operations—The item of net surplus on the ordinary balance sheet conveys little or nothing to the general reader or executive unless consideration is given to the items which have been deducted from the gross surplus. Ordinarily common and preferred dividends are the first items given consideration after which come special dividends and general reserves such as were set up during the recent period of adjustment.

Unless these items are taken into consideration it is difficult to realize the large amounts which might have been included in surplus at the end of a year, and whether or not the earnings are sufficient to meet the dividend requirements alone.

The figures represented on Chart No. 13 when put in the form of a balance sheet never could convey as this chart does, the effect of the deductions from surplus in the years 1921 and 1922. Had such a chart been in use, the fallacy of paying common dividends the first three months of 1922 would have been realized, when as clearly shown, the surplus account was forty-five hundred dollars less at the end of the year 1921 than it was at the beginning.

Such charges as this to surplus are what have put many shortsighted organizations on the rocks.

By analyzing in this way the executive sees well in advance the trend of the surplus account.

Analysis of $1 Sales Values— The graphic analysis of the component parts of what really constitutes a sale, furnishes a comparison that it is not possible to obtain by the use of figures alone. The accumulation of the various elements of a $1 sale as shown on Chart No. 14 brings out clearly and concisely the relative value of these

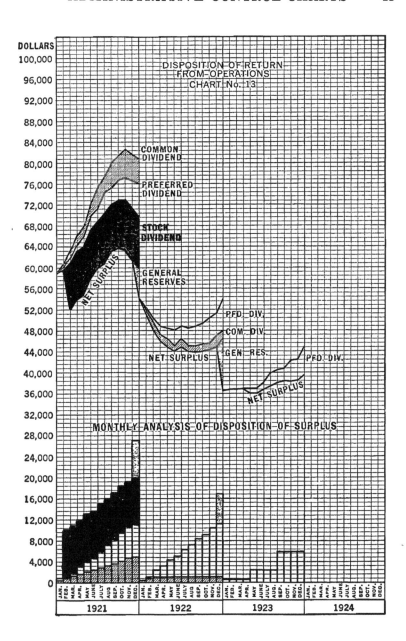

factors. It is really measuring proportionately the various items in an Income Statement to show what proportions are consumed by Manufacturing expenses, Selling expenses and General Administration expenses as well as the balance represented by surplus.

On Chart No. 14 is shown that in Jan., Feb., and March, 1922 the cost of sales and selling expense exceeded the selling values. In addition, General Administrative Expense and Dividends were to be considered, resulting in a deficit of 26.25, 31.68 and 21.89 cents, respectively, on each dollar of sales. At the close of the same year, as a result of extraordinary adjustment, cost of sales was reduced from 69.78 to 37.30 cents per dollar of sales in one month, giving a surplus of 25.70 cents on a dollar in December.

By virtue of the common basis being $1, the figures in the chart are automatically on a percentage basis:

Example	Jan. 1, 1920	July, 1922
Cost of Sales per $1	$ .6106 or 61%	$ .7766
Selling Expenses per $1	.1210	.1687
Gen. Admin. Exp. per $1	.1301	.1104
Dividends	.0162	.0330
	$ .8779	$1.0887
Leaving a surplus of	.1221	Leaving a deficit— .0887
	$1.00	$1.00

The Dollar Analysis of Sales, Chart No. 14, tells the story of operations and transactions not only for a limited period, but for a series of periods.

The following salient points to be emphasized in the ordinary income statement are illustrated in a way impossible by figures or statements:

1. The Cost of goods sold per every dollar of Sales.
2. The margin of gross profit realized on each dollar of sales.
3. The selling expenses on each dollar of sales.

4. The net operating profit on each dollar of sales.
5. The amount of administration expenses per each dollar of sales.
6. The amount of dividend absorbed per each dollar of sales.
7. The surplus per each dollar of sales.

While the amounts shown on the Income Statement of sales, expenses, and surplus are interesting, it is the relationships of and between these items which are really important.

Another important feature of visualizing the dollar value of sales is that it brings out any extraordinary adjustments in the various accounts which would ordinarily be lost in a mass of figures and would not be discovered before an audit was made. These adjustments are extremely prominent as shown on the accompanying chart for the month of December, 1922, when the cost of sales dropped from 69.78 cents per dollar in November to 37.30 cents per dollar.

It is physically impossible for an executive to remember from month to month the various costs of sales and such adjustments would ordinarily "get by," but when he sees such a drastic reduction in any account, his curiosity is immediately aroused and a further investigation results.

In this particular instance the cost of sales was reduced in the month of December by an adjustment of Depreciation sufficient not only to overcome the deficit for the first eleven months but to show a small profit for the year.

It is seen by the red area on the chart at December 1922 that in this month a greater profit is shown than in any month for the preceding three years; also that the cost of sales was decidedly less in this than in any previous month. It would seem extraordinary if this condition actually existed and the executive naturally looks for further

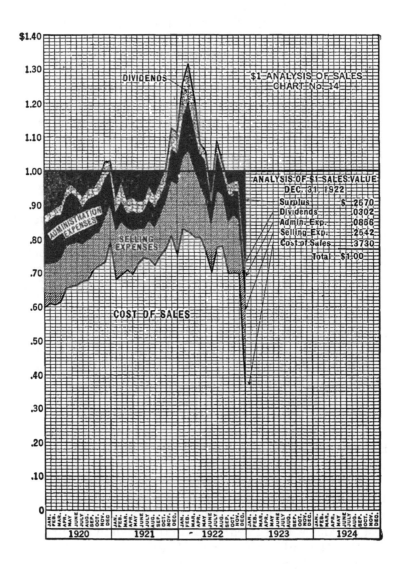

verification. He immediately refers to his Cost of Production charts, showing Material, Labor and Overhead costs per pound monthly and he sees that the answer is in a Depreciation adjustment.

All this is done in a few minutes and the executive is armed with actual facts and a mental impression of what this adjustment actually was and means.

Sales by Commodities or Departments— By showing the commodity sales, or sales of each department, independently, the executive is in a position to see what commodities should be pushed and to what extent his expectations are being fulfilled, thus giving him a clearer understanding of his business results.

He has a panoramic view of sales activities, not only by months but by periods and he is equipped to measure independently the relative selling strength of each department or commodity.

Seasonal variations may be quickly seen and extraordinary conditions realized.

For example, an examination of the month of January shows that each year, in most instances, sales have decreased in comparison with December, while in June the condition is reversed, Chart No. 15.

Charts Nos. 15 and 16 allow for comparison between individual months, the same month in past years, and show the seasonal fluctuations of each department.

They may be used for extending in pencil estimates of future business or sales quotas, and a comparison between estimated and actual as they are reported.

Sales and Cost of Sales— Since Cost of Sales or Cost of Production, as it is sometimes called, represents the greater portion of the deductions from income from Sales, it is a decided advantage to have these items compared as on Charts Nos. 17 and 18.

The upper line shows the monthly variations in Sales;

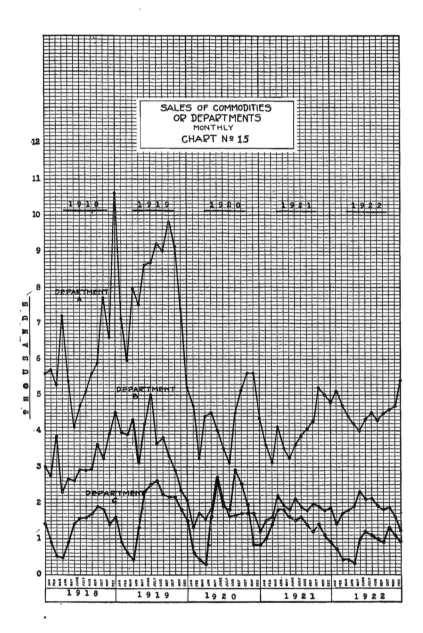

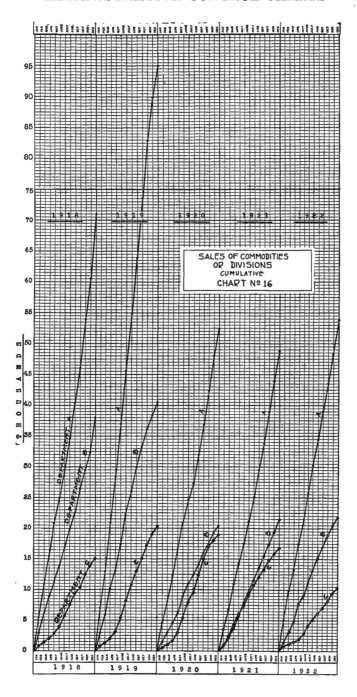

SALES OF COMMODITIES
OR DIVISIONS
CUMULATIVE
CHART № 16

the lower line shows the Cost of Sales, or Cost of Production, and on Chart No. 17 is shown the cents of cost, per one dollar of Sales. The latter also represents the percentage of Cost of Sales to Sales, since 100 cents equal a dollar and 100 per cent equals the whole.

Contrary to the theory of large scale production, the proportionate values of cost of sales increased during the first two years. In other words, where sales were increased, likewise was the cost of sales, thereby reducing the gross profit. When sales were increased from $16,600 in March, 1918, to $20,800 in October, 1918, the costs increased from $10,200 to $14,900, or from 61.4 cents to 71.8 cents per dollar of sales.

No ordinary report would bring out this vital information and only by visualization are these facts brought out.

Another point of interest is the decided drop in Cost of Sales in June and December, 1920. These dates are the semi-annual and annual accounting periods and it is not unlikely that they are a result of adjustments. As such they indicate the necessity of closely checking the cost reports.

Sales and Profit—Charts Nos. 19 and 20 visualize two of the most important elements of the Income Statement, and since every business man knows what these titles mean it would be useless to go into lengthy discussion or detail.

However, it is desirable to show the individual and cumulative values on the charts.

It was shown on Chart No. 17 that during the years 1919 and 1920 the cost per dollar of sales was greatest and consequently during these years the profit showed a decided decrease. Also, that for the first four months in the year 1921, the gross profit, represented by the margin between the upper and lower lines on Chart No. 17, was insufficient to cover the additional expenses, resulting in a deficit.

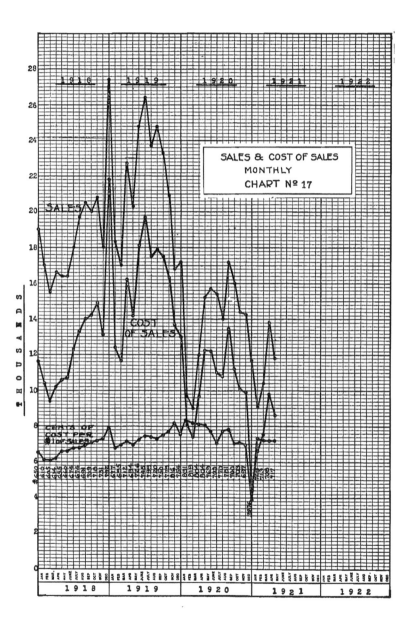

SALES & COST OF SALES
MONTHLY
CHART Nº 17

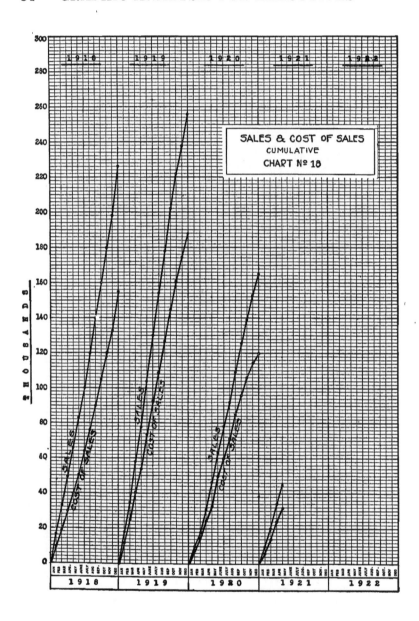

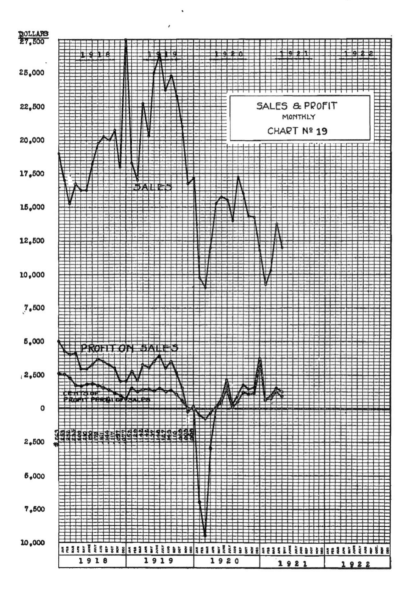

SALES & PROFIT
MONTHLY
CHART Nº 19

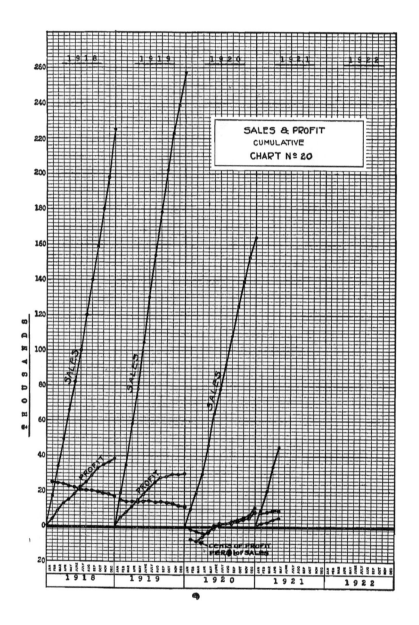

A similar condition is shown on Chart No. 14 (Dollar Analysis of Sales) in 1922 when administration and a portion of the selling expenses were above the line representing a $1 sales value.

The range between these two items makes it almost impossible to memorize their relative values and one would never think that the monthly fluctuations represented such extreme variations as shown by the line, on Chart No. 19, indicating cents of net operating profit per $1 of sales.

It is readily seen that the increase in sales did not result in an increase of profits but that in the year 1918 the increase in Sales resulted in a continued decrease in profits.

Analysis of Profit and Loss and Sales— The volume of annual profit or loss for each class of merchandise or department, as well as a cross-section of the total business is shown on Chart No. 21.

The horizontal scale shows the volume of sales expressed as a percentage of the total sales and the vertical scale shows the percentage of net operating profit or loss.

Obviously, commodity or department C is by far the most profitable for with only 16% of the total sales, the return in profit was 52% of the total, or about $65,000.

On the other hand, commodity or department D was most unprofitable, having sustained a loss in net operating profit although the sales were 25% of the total. The loss amounted to 15% or $18,750 and it is a speculation as to the probable results had some of the sales effort used in D been apportioned to A, B or C. The analysis of sales effort and opportunity outlined in Chapter III furnishes a means of accurately determining this.

The conditions are immediately brought out with little effort on the part of the reader. No simpler or more effective means could be used to present this analysis to

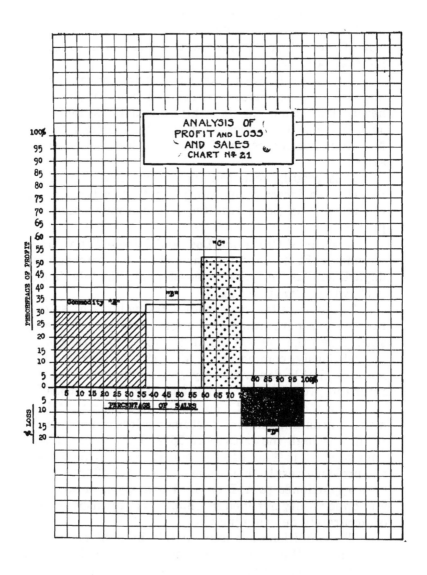

the busy executive. The results, both in sales and net operating profit, of each commodity or department are all on a common basis and at a glance the user sees and absorbs more than he could get from many minutes of reading figures only.

Summary Sheet—The Summary Sheet classifies the Balance Sheet and Income Statement item by item and summarizes what was shown on the charts for the current month or any number of months that may be incorporated in the statement.

It tabulates the various items and may be used for reference or comment when it is inadvisable to distribute the charts.

It contains the items shown on the charts with the chart reference number on the left hand side.

ANALYSIS OF BALANCE SHEET
AND INCOME STATEMENT

Chart No.		JANUARY Actual Condition Figures	FEBRUARY Actual Condition Figures	MARCH Actual Condition Figures
1-2	Current Assets	$133,404	$135,350	$138,064
	Current Liabilities	49,184 $2.71	51,107 $2.65	53,023 $2.60

This signifies the dollars of Current Assets for every dollar of Current Liabilities (Good Business Balance).

| 2-3 | Cash | 12,927 | 12,672 | 12,817 |
| - | Current Liabilities | 49,184 .26 | 51,107 .25 | 53,023 .24 |

This signifies that there has been an average of 25 cents in cash for every dollar of Current Liabilities.

| - 4 | Accts. Receivable | 39,178 | 40,799 | 42,803 |
| | Sales | 9,090 4.31 | 10,387 3.93 | 13,883 3.08 |

Shows the condition of Accounts Receivable each month in proportion to $1 of sales.

Jan. Accounts Receivable equals 73 days sales
Feb.   "   "   "   "   77   "   "
Mar.   "   "   "   "   80   "   "

THIS WOULD INDICATE THAT COLLECTIONS ARE SLOW.

| 5-6 | Sales | 9,090 | 10,387 | 13,883 |
| | Materials & Supplies — Including Goods in Process | 25.773 .35 | 25,193 .41 | 25,317 .55 |

Indicates the cents of Sales for each dollar tied up in Material & Supplies & Goods in Process.

5-6 Sales 9,090   10,387   13,883
    Finished Goods .... 52,318 .17 53,427 .19 53,819 .26
    This shows the cents of Sales for each Dollar of Finished
    Goods. Jan. Finished Goods equals 5.8 Months Sales. Feb.
    equals 5.1 Months Sales. March equals 3.9 Months Sales.
5-6 Sales   9,090   10,387   13,883
    Total Inventory.. ...... 78,092 .116 78,621 .13 79,136 .18
    Slow turnover of Finished Goods tends to make the propor-
    tion of sales to Total Inventory too small.
  7 Sales 9,090   10,387   13,883
    Property & Plant
        Investment .... 186,449 .049 186,531 .06 186,668 .07
    This signifies that there were 5, 6 and 7 cents of Sales for
    every dollar of Property & Plant Investment. Volume of
    sales is much too small for the Plant Investment.
8-9 Reserves 17,012   17,276   17,542
    Total Assets ... . 338,963 .05 341.152 .05 343,680 .05
    This indicates 5 cents of Reserves for each dollar of Total
    Assets.
 10 Fixed Liabilities 126,347   133,089   129,443
    Surplus 55,799 2.26 55,847 2.38 56,429 2.29
    Shows that borrowed capital exceeds earned capital by more
    than a ratio of 2 to 1.
 11 Profit or Loss........ ..   187   48   582
    Capitalization .... 146,387 .001 146,387 .0003 146,387 .004
    Indicates the cents, profit or loss for each $1 of capitalization
    at which the operations were conducted.

Wall Charts— Development of organizations has necessitated various committees to discuss collectively the
affairs of the organization and with them the demand for a
larger type of chart commonly known as the Wall Chart.
For such committees wall charts are invaluable, for with
their broad problems of numerous factors, charts materially simplify the discussion. They present the data in a
language common to all, leaving no room for misinterpre-
tation. Every one starts at the same point with the same
idea. In other words, the minds are assembled at a common level and are concentrated on the data represented by
the chart. The variations are registered unconsciously
and an intelligent discussion is effected.

These committees assemble to think out policies and
plans, to study the operation of policies and plans, analyze
organization, administrative efficiency, financial budgets,
sales, production and competition. Every minute of their

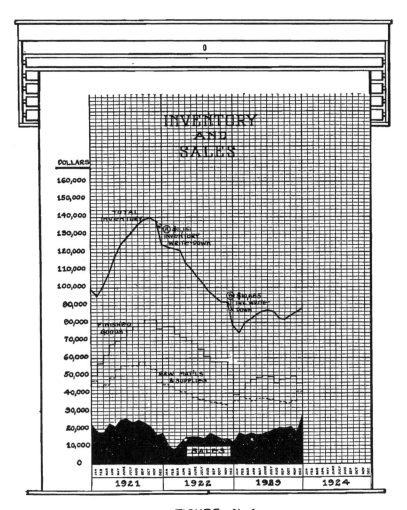

FIGURE No.1

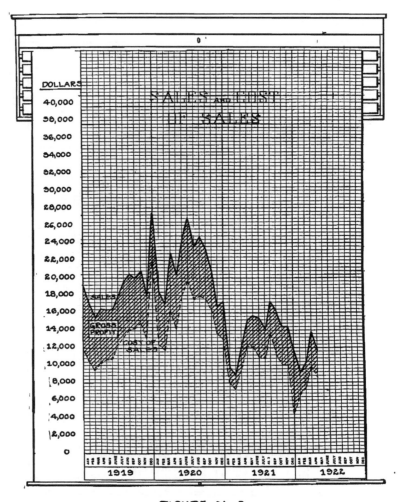

FIGURE No. 2

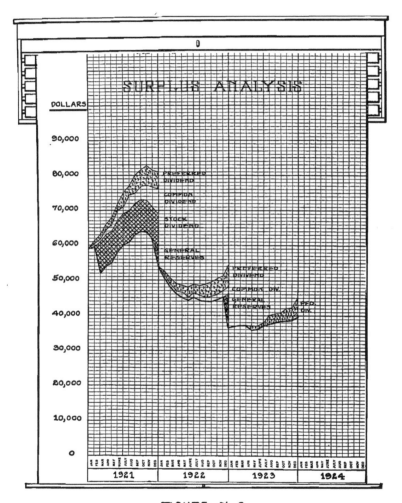

FIGURE No.3

time is valuable and any time lost lessens the efficiency and value of the committee.

With wall charts the committee can sit at their table and discuss definitely, without reference to any figures, the various phases of the business shown.

These charts can be made in various sizes to be mounted on rollers that operate like a shade and are encased in a wooden roll-front map case.

CHAPTER III

SALES CHARTS

Sales Charts— Charts may be used to great advantage in selling an idea to salesmen. Here is an actual occurrence that demonstrates the feasibility of the use of charts in elucidating an apparently somewhat involved idea.

The chief executive of a shoe jobbing house found that the sales in four departments were badly out of balance—that 33% of sales were made from Dept. A, 13% from Dept. B, 24% from Dept. C and 30% from Dept. D.

An opportunity to increase the sales in Depts. A, B and C was not apparent but it was obvious that the sales in Dept. D. should be larger, as explained hereafter.

No analysis of individual salesmen's sales had been made at this time but the executive, realizing that salesmen's effort is the source of total volume, determined to analyze the sales of two salesmen and compare the proportionate sales of each with the total average. He selected the sales of the best two men.

When the figures were handed to him they looked as follows:

	DEPT. A	DEPT. B	DEPT. C	DEPT. D
Total Sales	33%	13%	24%	30%
Salesman No. 1	33%	18%	28%	21%
" " 2	19%	15%	46%	20%

He at once observed that both of these salesmen were selling only about two-thirds of what they should sell of

65

Dept. D merchandise to equal the total average.

A little further figuring developed the fact that if salesmen Nos. 1 and 2 could maintain their sales in departments where they equaled or exceeded the total average and bring their sales up to the total average in departments where they were low, salesman No. 1 would increase his sales 9% and salesman No. 2, his sales 19%. This truly was an invitation worth considering, a mark worth shooting at, so it was decided to make an analysis of sales of other salesmen, traveling in analogous territory.

Reports were called for on nine salesmen's territories. The report when received looked like this:

	DEPT. A	DEPT. B	DEPT. C	DEPT. D
Total Sales	33%	13%	24%	30%
Salesman No. 1	33%	18%	28%	21%
" " 2	19%	15%	46%	20%
" " 3	48%	6%	18%	28%
" " 4	48%	10%	16%	26%
" " 5	28%	22%	12%	38%
" " 6	14%	10%	16%	60%
" " 7	45%	10%	30%	15%
" " 8	28%	12%	24%	36%
" " 9	25%	20%	28%	27%

These figures were a revelation. They showed a lack of balance that was astounding, possibilities undreamed of. A composite of the work of the best salesmen in each department indicated a possible increase of 76% in the total business.

The question to be solved was how to make the problem clear to nine salesmen who must be influenced.

As it was apparent that figures mean little to minds not trained to figures, it was decided to make a chart, graphically presenting the lack of balance in the various salesmen's sales. Chart No. 22 was the result.

A careful study of this chart is worth while. The first column indicates percentage of total sales made in each of the four departments.

Columns 1 to 9 indicate sales of nine salesmen.
The Total Sales column is not drawn to scale and
indicates only percentages.

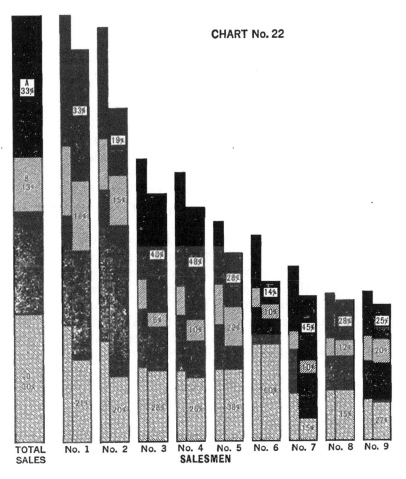

CHART No. 22

TOTAL SALES   No. 1   No. 2   No. 3   No. 4   No. 5   No. 6   No. 7   No. 8   No. 9

SALESMEN

Columns 1 to 9 are drawn to scale. The difference
in the length of the right-hand division of each column
shows the difference in the total pairs of shoes sold by

each of the nine salesmen.

The difference in the total volume of each salesman may be attributed to a difference in the size of territory covered.

A reference to columns 1 and 2 will simplify the reading of the chart.

It will be noted that 21% of No. 1's total sales were made on D merchandise whereas 60% of the sales of No. 6 were made on D.

No. 1 sold 33% of A whereas No. 6 sold but 14%.

Now note the left division of column No. 1 and column No. 6. If No. 1 had maintained his sales on A, B and C and brought his sales on D up to 30% of his total sales, he would have increased his total sales 9%.

If No. 6 maintained his sales on D and increased his sales to equal the average on A, B and C, he would increase his total sales 19%.

The difference in the length of the left-hand and right-hand divisions of each column indicates the amount that each salesman would increase his sales if he maintained his sales at the high places and increased his sales to equal the average at the low places.

This chart may add nothing to the information of the man who has facility in reading figures but to the salesman who has not it is very illuminating. He views it from an entirely different angle and it awakens in his mind an interest which figures never would.

This chart was submitted to the nine salesmen whose figures were used.

Numerals were used instead of names so that no salesman would be able to more than guess which column represented his sales. A decision to do this was in accord with the house policy.

An interesting incident occurred during the explanation of the chart that brought out clearly the effect it had upon the minds of the salesmen.

One of them, after studying the chart for a few minutes, said to the executive who was conducting the meeting: "I notice that 60% of the sales of No. 6 were made on D and that his sales in the other three departments are very small. Does it occur to you that No. 6 specializes on D?"

"It is obvious he does," replied the executive, "and that's exactly what we want to avoid. We do not want him to devote less energy to D but we want him to devote more to A, B and C. By specializing on D he sacrifices his opportunity on A, B and C."

Then he said this:

"When we employ a salesman and assign to him a territory we place in his hands an opportunity. Although we hand that opportunity to him it still belongs to us. We cannot surrender our interest.

"There is a certain crop to be gathered in each territory. The crop is ours. We are willing to pay to have it picked but we must be sure that it is picked clean.

"Salesman No. 6 has done good work in picking D merchandise. He has done poor work in picking A, B and C.

"Salesman No. 6 who apparently specializes on D, may not be qualified to pick the A, B and C crop. If he admits this it may be necessary for us to put a specialist to work on A, B and C."

Then directing his attention to the salesman who had provoked the retort, he asked: "How would you feel if we put a specialist on your territory to pick the crops where you do not pick clean?"

"I wouldn't like it," was the reply.

The executive, again referring to the chart, said this: "These columns indicate something more than pairs sold— they indicate profits earned by salesmen. As you all sell on commission, increased sales mean increased compensation. When you increase your sales 9% or 19% you increase your income 9% or 19%."

It was not a new idea, not a new argument, but presented in a new way it drove home the point the executive wanted to make.

Another incident was called to the attention of the writer where a corporation had made a large appropriation to be expended in national advertising with a view to influencing the public to bring pressure to bear upon dealers and thus stimulate the demand for the product.

It was the opinion of a sales promotion specialist that this money might be more wisely spent in other directions and he proceeded to illustrate the reasons for his opinion with graphic charts.

By means of these charts it was shown that there were weak places in the selling plan, trade opportunities undeveloped, and that until these weak places were strengthened and opportunities fully developed, money expended in general advertising would prove wasteful and unwise.

As an example an investigation was made of conditions in six selected branches. This investigation was strictly confined to selling and did not consider the product although it is obvious that the quality and price as compared to competitors have a vital influence on sales. It was also assumed that the products were equal or superior to any offered by competitors in quality, price and variety and that the service rendered compared favorably.

These six branches had a total of approximately 2,900 actual and prospective customers for the previous year and they divided them into the three classes:

A.   Those who use the commodities exclusively. Of these there were 613.

B.   Those who use the commodities for only a small portion of their requirements. Of these there were 1,602.

C. Those who use the commodities in question but are not listed in either of the above classes of customers. Of these there were 683.

The following statistics show the comparative proportion of the three classes of customers, not only of the combined territory made up of the six branches, but also in each of the individual branches. These figures show that 613 class A customers bought 23,102 units, an average of 37.7 per customer and that 1,602 class B customers bought 16,030 units, an average of 10 per customer.

If units in the same proportion were sold to class B customers as were sold to class A customers the unit sales would be increased 100%.

	CLASS A			CLASS B			CLASSES A & B			CLASS C
Br.	Cus-tomers	Unit Sales	Av.	Cus-tomers	Unit Sales	Av.	Cus-tomers	Unit Sales	Av.	
1	113	5,599	49.6	714	4,752	6.6	827	10,351	12 5	95
2	82	2,555	31.2	119	1,022	8 6	201	3,577	17 8	216
3	52	1,669	32.0	157	1,781	11 3	209	3,450	16 5	111
4	156	5,662	36 3	229	3,506	15.3	385	9,168	24 0	98
5	127	5,048	39.7	332	3,362	10.1	459	8,410	18 3	158
6	83	2,569	30.9	51	1,607	31.5	134	4,176	31.1	5
Total	613	23,102	37.7	1,602	16,030	10.0	2,215	39,132	17.6	683

It is obvious from these figures that of the total customers in the combined territory over 50% are in class B, that is, they are not regular purchasers; that about 25% are in class C and do not purchase at all, and that the regular or class A customers represent only about 30% of the total of classes A and B. This means that 1 in every 3 customers purchases these commodities exclusively.

This is more clearly illustrated on Chart No. 23 where the comparative proportions of the three classes of customers in the individual branches and the combined total are represented on the Circular Percentage Chart.

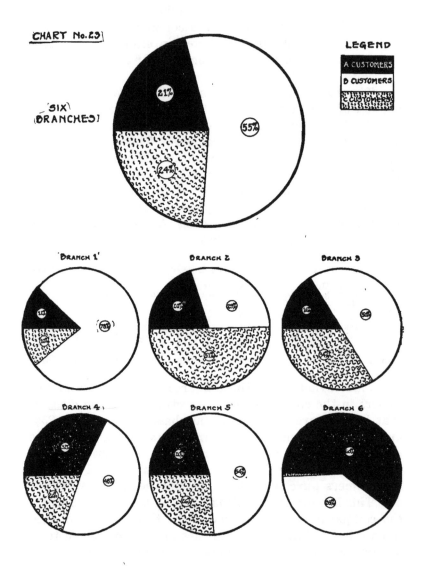

CHART No.24

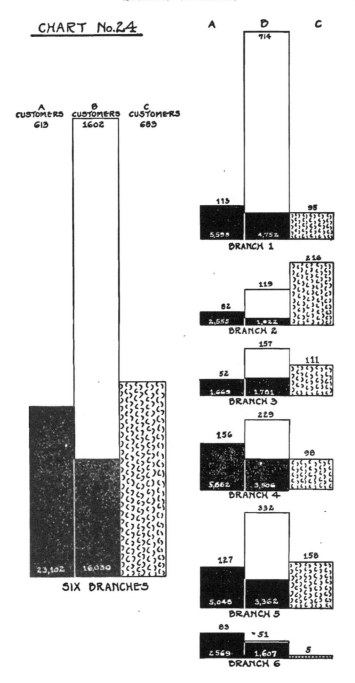

A
CUSTOMERS
613

B
CUSTOMERS
1602

C
CUSTOMERS
689

A   D   C
714

113   95
5,599   4,752
BRANCH 1

216
119
82
2,555   1,622
BRANCH 2

157
52   111
1,669   1,701
BRANCH 3

229
156
98
5,662   3,506
BRANCH 4

332
127   158
5,048   3,362
BRANCH 5

83   51
5
2,569   1,607
BRANCH 6

23,102   16,030
SIX BRANCHES

The individual branch circles show that Branches 4 and 6 are more highly developed in class A customers than the others and that Branches 1 and 5 have an excess of class B customers.

To more clearly illustrate the situation Chart No. 24 was submitted showing the comparative number of classes A, B and C customers in actual figures.

In the large diagram on the right representing the six branches the three columns represent the number of A, B and C customers in the combined territories. The figures at the bottom indicate the number of units sold.

An examination of Chart No. 24 shows a marked difference in the proportions of the three classes of customers in these six branches. Branch 6 has only five class C customers in its territory, while Branch No. 5 has 158, No. 4 has 98, No. 1 has 95, No. 2 has 216 and No. 3 has 111.

The object of this chart was to point out to the branch managers the necessity of studying their respective conditions carefully and determining whether or not more intensive selling methods could be adopted.

Note that the black column at the extreme left, representing class A customers, is shorter than either the plain white column representing class B customers or the shaded column representing class C customers, which indicates that only a small portion of the possible sales was made. The same plan was carried out in each of the smaller sections, representing the respective branches, so that the undeveloped opportunity, indicated by the white columns, was seen at a glance.

The excess of undeveloped territory in the combined area and in the respective branches is clearly shown by this chart. Note the preponderance of undeveloped territory in Branch No. 1 as compared to Branch No. 6.

These charts so completely convinced the executives

CHART No. 25

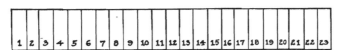

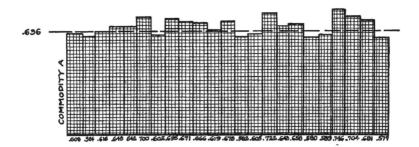

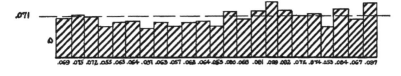

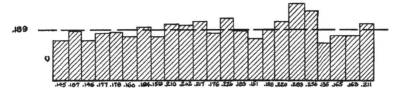

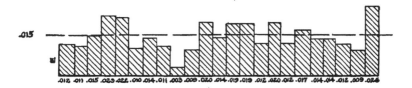

of the lack of balance in the branch sales that they requested a further investigation of the condition of four commodities the sales of which they were particularly anxious to increase.

Chart No. 25 was then introduced to show the sales by branches and commodities and it shows the same lack of balance indicated on Charts Nos. 23 and 24.

23 branches are indicated at the top of the chart and in the columns below are shown the volumes of commodities sold by each of the branches in their respective classes.

In each commodity a broken line indicates the average sales of all the branches and where the top of the branch column falls below this line poor sales are indicated in that branch. The space between the broken line and the top of the column in every instance indicates undeveloped opportunity.

This chart instantaneously shows that the fluctuations between branch sales of commodity A are not nearly so great as in the other commodities. This would indicate that more time and effort was expended by the salesmen on commodity A, resulting in their neglecting commodities B, C, D and E.

Visualizing the condition in this way enabled the executives to see instantly that the greatest variations in sales between branches appeared in commodities D and E, that Branch No. 8 exceeded the average sales in commodity A but was below the average in the sales of all other commodities, whereas Branch No. 23 sales were below the average in commodity A and equal to or above the average in the others.

An analysis of the salesmen's effort is shown on Chart No. 26 and indicates a greater lack of balance than there was in the branches. Chart No. 26 follows the same general arrangement as Chart No. 25, and a comparison of these two charts gives a better understanding of the conditions.

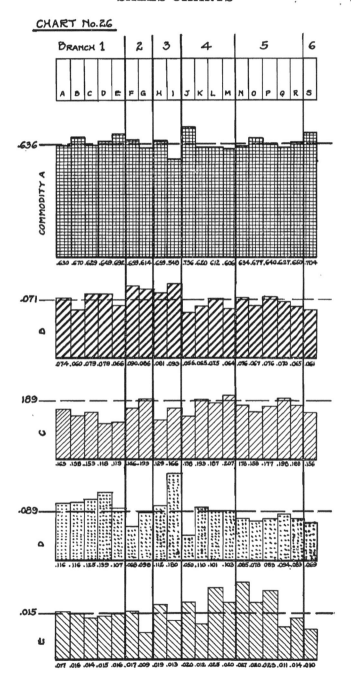

The letters from A to S at the top represent the 19 salesmen employed in the six branches.

As on Chart No. 25, the broken line indicates the average sales of each commodity and it will be noted that some salesmen are far below the average in some commodities and far above in others.

The object of this chart was to show the comparative results obtained in the different commodities by the salesmen in these six branches, and it more than served its purpose.

Consider salesman J; he is far above the average on commodities A and E and far below the average on B, C and D, whereas salesman G is below the average on commodities A and E and above the average on the other three commodities.

A further analysis of the salesmen's work in the six branches is shown on Chart No. 27, where the territory of each salesman is considered. It shows a marked difference in the amount of territory covered by the various salesmen.

In this instance the word territory was applied to customers rather than to geographical territory.

This chart clearly shows the preponderance of customers alloted to salesman D (212), and the comparatively few assigned to salesmen Q and R (48). This means that salesman D has to see nearly five times as many customers as either Q or R. The chart shows not only the class A and C customers that make up a salesman's territory but it shows the number of class B customers as well.

It is interesting to note that in most instances where a salesman has a comparatively large number of customers assigned to him he has a small number of class A customers. This may be because it is impossible for him to give to any an amount of service that would develop his

CHART No.27

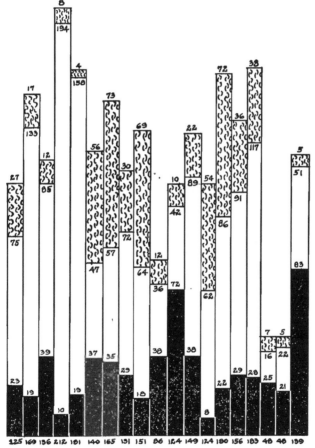

TOTAL   CUSTOMERS

LEGEND

territory as it should be developed.

These charts so clearly illustrated the conditions that all thoughts of general advertising were dismissed and an intensive study was made of the company's merchandising policies and conditions.

CHAPTER IV

COST CHARTS

Costs— The matter of compilation of cost reports for executives has always been a problem presenting difficulties as to the manner in which they should be set forth, so that important information will be conveyed quickly and with sufficient emphasis, and the unimportant points given less prominence.

Costs are almost always figured on some sort of unit of production—pounds, feet, gallons, number of items produced, etc. In many cases where these unit costs do not run higher than 3, 4, 5, 6, 8, or 10c per unit, a variation of half or three-quarters of a cent appears too small to command much attention, yet a half cent represents an increase of 5% on a 10c article, or 10% on a 5c article. If a business is earning 10%, such an increase of cost on a 10c article will eat up 50% of the profit, and in the case of the 5c article, will consume the entire profit. One method of endeavoring to emphasize the full significance of variations of this kind, apparently small, which really represent large comparative variations in low priced goods, has been to present figures covering 100 units instead of only one unit, but even in doing this, a figure showing a cost of $10.50 for 100 articles which are expected to cost but $10, is not enough different to incite any great concern on the part of the responsible executive, who is perhaps under pressure requiring more immediate action in some other direction.

81

Such figures do not command attention in proportion to their importance to a business. The aim and purpose of all reports, including costs, is to present the salient points of the story of the operations of a business in a manner to conserve the time of the busy executive, and charts provide the means of recording costs in a way which will show each half-cent or quarter-cent as great or as small as is its importance to the figures to which it is related. In making this representation on a chart each unit of variation in cost, up or down, is fixed at a measure or distance which will give to the observer whatever impression of the change is considered necessary to command attention in proportion to the importance of the fluctuation represented. For example, if a fluctuation of one quarter of a cent is of just as vital importance, in the cost or selling price of one article, as one cent is in the price of some other article, your chart may be so planned that the upward or downward trend represented by the quarter of a cent will be one inch, while in the case of the other cost fluctuation of equal importance, the measure of this one cent fluctuation may also be set at one inch, thus bringing them on a parity and eliminating the necessity for mental processes of comparison. This illustrates the adaptability and elasticity of charts as compared with figures.

Charts covering costs lead the observer out of the maze and fog of figures and show a line, or two lines, or three lines, leading up or down according to whether the trend of the costs is upward or downward. The terms "uphill" and "downhill" are of common usage in expressing the condition of a business, and charts are planned so that they show the hills and valleys of a business and are comparable to standing out in the open and looking at the horizon. Perspective is there, and a broad clear view with sharp lines of demarcation, showing the commanding "peaks." This result is obtained merely by the

position of the various points on the chart, making it unnecessary even to look at the figures to determine whether
a specific figure is a "2" or a "3," or an "8" or a "9." The
points on the chart exhibit this, by the angle of the line,
without necessitating the mental process of considering
whether a figure is greater or less than another. These
lines which form the "horizon," so to speak, run either up
or down, indicating increase or decrease—greater or smaller costs.

Costs, usually made up of three major elements, are
of special interest as to how these elements combine into
a total cost, and the lines of these three elements, material,
labor and overhead, should be charted with the total costs,
thus correlating each of them with the total cost and with
one another.

Charts 28 and 28A show a comparison of Units of
Production and Cost of Production. No. 28, on plain ruling, gives a correct picture of the variations in actual
quantities while No. 28A, on ratio ruling, shows the variations in terms of percent. On the ratio chart equal percentage differences are represented by equal vertical dis-
tances. A constant percentage of increase or decrease will
plot as a straight line and the slope (or angle) of the line
is a measure of the rate of increase or decrease.

SUMMARY OF COSTS IN DOLLARS

	Production In Pounds	Cost of Material	Cost of Labor	Cost of Overhead	Total Cost of Production
January	735,000	433,797	49,833	53,067	536,697
February	709,200	390,556	55,530	58,864	504,950
March	432,000	296,698	33,437	29,246	359,381
April	525,000	346,973	50,925	43,680	441,578
May	501,000	354,107	46,743	47,795	448,645
June	730,260	548,279	67,111	59,078	674,468
July	720,296	620,535	66,771	77,360	764,666
August	708,000	543,886	54,374	50,834	649,094
September	480,000	352,368	33,840	36,864	423,072
October	720,300	504,066	58,272	67,492	629,830
November	830,000	668,565	79,016	55,693	803,274
December	824,600	583,157	80,069	67,535	730,761

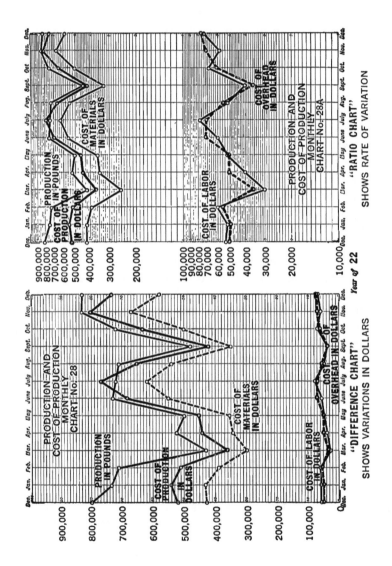

It is a fact well worth remark that the charting of these three elements by separate lines, together with the line showing total cost, which they combine to make up, gives a most complete insight into cost and sets forth these elements in such a way that their flow and fluctuation remain fixed in the executive's mind more definitely and permanently than by any other means yet devised. Their continuity from month to month is also an extremely valuable factor, showing, as it does, a simultaneous comparison with all other preceding months, wherein lies virtually the greatest value of cost figures—comparison. The completeness of the past record also spreads before you splendid information by which to gauge and estimate future costs and volume of business, as the upward and downward flow of these lines indicates that they will have a related upward and downward flow in future.

The foregoing comments on costs have been confined almost exclusively to unit costs, but there is also the matter of records of complete costs to which such charts lend themselves equally well, that is, a line embracing the total cost of all sales in connection with which may be charted the total income from all sales; thus the space between the two represents profit or loss. Such a chart may be designed covering the grand total of all sales as stated, or it may be subdivided into departments, or products, or territories, or any other classification.

This form of chart is illustrated in Chapter II. Here again their value lies in the continuity of their story. In making up these cost charts, showing a line for overhead, a line for labor, and a line for material, there is put graphically before the observer the relative importance of these three factors in the total cost, and the share which each of these major cost elements represents in the total cost. Chart No. 29 is a chart covering the cost per pound of goods produced by a manufacturing company over a period of 24 months. You will note that there are twenty-four points on the black line, each of these representing the overhead cost for a month, and a corresponding num-

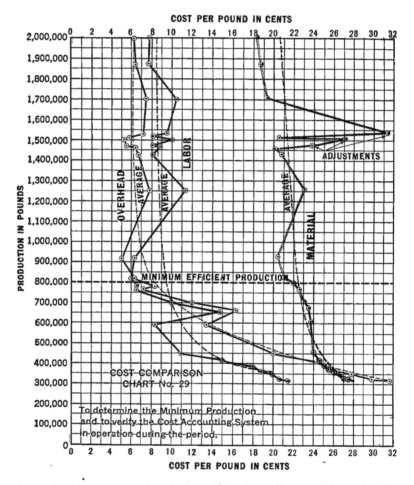

ber of points on each of the other two lines—labor (red) and material (green). The chart is laid out with production scale in pounds running vertically, from the lowest production at the bottom to the highest production at the top of the sheet. It is made up by taking two years' production and costs therefor and arranging them, not chronologically but according to the number of pounds produced. Thus is obtained definite information of the effect of volume on cost, and also which of the three factors, labor, material and overhead, shows the greatest fluctuation due to volume of production. No proof need be offered of the value of such information.

Overhead cost per pound is affected by volume more radically than either of the other two elements, since, as will be observed, it fluctuates from 6c per pound on a production of two million pounds, to 31.8c per pound on a production of three hundred seventeen thousand pounds. Similarly, the line covering labor cost per pound, follows the burden cost per pound very closely, but the labor cost per pound does not decrease as rapidly in inverse ratio to production as does the burden cost per pound. You will observe by following the 800,000 lb. line across the chart, that just above this 800,000 lb. line the cost of labor per pound becomes, for the first time, greater than the cost of overhead per pound, and remains at a greater cost per pound from that point on up, whereas, below the 800,000 lb. production line the contrary is true; i. e., the cost of labor per pound becomes less than the cost of overhead per pound. Thus, automatically, this chart sets forth the information that 800,000 pounds production marks a dividing line or what may be termed a limit of minimum efficiency. Not only does it mark the point of production at which the labor cost per pound shows a sharp increase, but overhead cost per pound as well, and from that point downward, the overhead cost per pound shows even greater increases than labor costs.

The material line (green) gives information of a little different sort.

This element of cost in its very nature, can not fluctuate much in the amount consumed in producing a pound or a unit of a given kind of product, whether 400,000 pounds or 2,000,000 pounds are produced. This being the case, the fluctuations in this material line therefore portray the difference in the price at which the raw material has been procured for use in manufacture, rather than a difference in material cost per pound because of increase or decrease in volume of production; nevertheless, the element of volume of production enters into this figure to some extent, depending somewhat upon the nature of the product, and in this respect it gives you what figures will not give, in that it will show any fluctuation due to difference in volume of production, if a fluctuation due to that factor does exist.

The dotted lines represent the "average" costs of each element at the various volumes of production and are particularly valuable for estimating purposes.

These three lines, labor, material and overhead, make up a correlated narrative telling, on a comparative basis, how the total cost is made up, of what it is made up, and, to a large degree, the reasons for the increases and decreases therein. This is accomplished with very little reference to figures, or to be more exact, with reference only to such figures as the points on the chart indicate are abnormal.

Having dealt with the application of charts designed on what we shall term a maximum-minimum basis, we will now present a chart designed on a chronological basis. Each of these two forms of charts has its individual value and separate field, the former being more of a retrospective and analytical record in that the period charted must have already elapsed before any part of the chart can be made up. It begins with the present and reaches backward as far as desired, with all of the information in hand arranged so that the lines or curves are placed on the chart in the order of their volume or quantity. Chart No. 29, described above, runs from minimum to maximum or low to high, whereas the chart we will now describe is designed to be made up from month to month, adding, immediately after the close of each month, the lines representing that month's activities, thus building up what may be termed a current record, as it portrays what is taking place currently and chronologically in a business. This chart in the case of manufacturing costs is ordinarily made up of the three lines representing the same three elements as the maximum-minimum charts, i. e., material, labor and overhead. But, as stated, these lines are built up by adding the respective sections or segments each month, to what is already on the chart, thus giving a continuous, related history of a business.

On Charts No. 30 and 30A, total cost per pound is shown for one year, month by month (the full black line). Then there are the three lines showing the cost of each of the three major elements, material, labor and overhead, which make up the total cost.

SUMMARY OF COST PER POUND OF PRODUCTION

	Production In Pounds	Cost per lb. Material	Cost per lb. Labor	Cost per lb. Overhead	Total Cost per Pound
January	735,000	$ .5902	$ .0678	$ .0722	$ .7302
February	709,200	.5507	.0783	.0830	.7120
March	432,000	.6868	.0774	.0677	.8319
April	525,000	.6609	.0970	.0832	.8411
May	501,000	.7068	.0933	.0954	.8955
June	730,260	.7508	.0919	.0809	.9236
July	720,296	.8615	.0927	.1074	1.0616
August	708,000	.7682	.0768	.0718	.9168
September	480,000	.7341	.0705	.0768	.8814
October	720,300	.6998	.0809	.0937	.8744
November	830,000	.8055	.0952	.0671	.9678
December	824,600	.7072	.0971	.0819	.8862

By way of setting forth to a limited degree something of what such a chart does, it will be noted that for the month of July the total cost is shown as $1.0616, of which $.8615 is material, $.0927 is labor, and $.1074 is overhead.

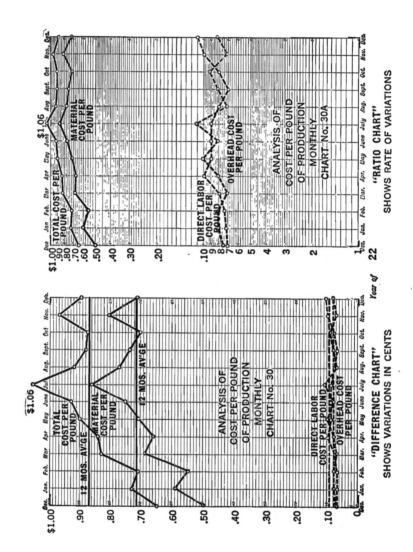

The month of August shows a sharp drop in the total cost per pound, which drop you will observe is almost as pronounced in the "material" line, indicating that almost the entire amount of this fluctuation is due to material, the remainder being shown by the fluctuation in the overhead line, and none of it being due to labor. This may be clearly seen without looking at figures at all, and, not alone this, but the eye is further attracted to the fact shown that immediately after the "total" and "material" lines show such a sharp rise (in July) they show an even sharper drop (in August). No reference to figures is needed to see this at a glance. This sharply ascending fluctuation, immediately followed by a sharply descending fluctuation, may mean one of several things not quite normal in the cost of material. It may mean a sudden rise in the cost of material followed by a sudden drop, or an error in the quantity or value of material charged to cost. In this particular instance, the most likely reason is the last named, i. e., an error in computation of cost. As a matter of fact, that proved to be the real reason for this apparent fluctuation. Before being charted it was passed over without being seen for the reason that this figure was but one of a list of 35 other costs for as many different plants of this organization, and it was lost in the crowd until the charting of it brought out emphatically the improbability of such a figure. This demonstrates in a small way, the value of such charts as a check or proof of the accuracy or inaccuracy of the compilation of cost figures. There are also several other high and low points on this chart which clearly showed the need of attention and investigation, but only after being charted. It also brings out very emphatically the fact that in this particular product the material used is by far the biggest factor of cost, and largely because of this the contour of the "Material" line follows very closely the contour of the "Total" line. On the other hand, it is just as apparent what part is supplied by labor and overhead in the cost of this product, both of these elements being not only smaller factors than material in the total cost, but being almost equal to each other, with slightly greater fluctuations in the cost of overhead per pound than in the cost of labor. This in turn brings us to the conclusion that labor is the factor most easily controlled in the cost of this product, material the most difficult to control, and overhead an intermediate factor. Thus are thrown out in strong relief the elements which warrant maximum attention.

The foregoing is confined almost entirely to records of unit costs of manufacture, and charts of this kind necessarily apply to a business which manufactures the products that it sells. There is also to be considered the business which buys its merchandise already manufactured and in a finished state, re-selling it as a jobber or wholesaler. Where a business consists of buying a completed product for re-sale, the concern engaged therein knows nothing of the material, labor or burden consumed in the manufacture of the product which it buys, and these items or elements are of no interest. The cost is that of the finished product, while the other major elements of operation consist of marketing costs only, without reference or relation to any manufacturing costs. The various subdivisions of selling expense are therefore of major importance in arriving at an analysis of operating expenses such as will provide a satisfactory control of marketing costs. These major elements consist to some degree of fixed charges such as rent, taxes, insurance, which remain "fixed" from month to month, neither increasing nor decreasing as a direct result of the volume or value of sales. A line is charted covering the total of these "fixed" expenses and by so doing they are eliminated from consideration as factors of operating cost susceptible of **ready** control, being obligations of such nature that the business must carry them in order to present its wares to the public. This line on a chart will show practically no variation from month to month, and its very contour therefore emphasizes its stability. If every factor in a business were as stable as this group, business would be less hazardous and there would be little need of either figures or charts. From this group we proceed to the other major factors of selling expense, which in the majority of business concerns consist of delivery costs, commission costs, if sales are on a commission basis, advertising, office staff salaries, traveling expenses of salesmen, and freight and cartage.

The charting of each of these lines gives a complete story of these respective kinds or classes of operating expense, exhibiting at a glance every fluctuation laid out before the observer in an unbroken narrative which, presented in this manner, relieves the mind of the burden of examining and analyzing rows and columns of figures.

The costs for this type of business are clearly and comprehensively analyzed by means of "Analysis of the Dollar Value of Sales" chart, No. 14, illustrated in Chapter II.

Stores Control—The use and value of charts starts at the receiving room door of a plant, on the arrival of material or merchandise. The keeping of a proper record of stock from the time of receiving it is one of the most important wheels in the machinery of a business. The store house or stock room is the source of supply of a business, and if this fails to produce the necessary raw material with which to keep busy the employees and the equipment of a concern, there is a consequent loss of both labor and overhead, together with loss of reputation and prestige with the customer or patron, as a result of inability to make prompt delivery of goods because of failure to have material on hand from which to produce the kind of goods needed to supply current demand. To permit a stock of some one kind of material to become depleted may mean, with a manufacturing concern, that some department of their factory, or possibly the entire factory, will be obliged to shut down, or for the sake of keeping the plant operating, some makeshift resorted to, such as producing goods not in demand, which goods after being produced may have to be kept in stock an unreasonably long time and the profit thereon dissipated because of the slow turnover. Therefore, when records of stock on hand are inadequate, or when they are carelessly or inaccurately kept permitting stocks to run down too low, or to become entirely exhausted, it is frequently necessary to resort to emergency measures which are costly and tend to disorganize a business.

The storehouse or stockroom is usually just a little more remote from the center of business activity than the producing parts of a plant, and because of this it is apt to come under the eye of the executive too infrequently for him to know just what is happening there. The stores charts come in here to pick up the storehouse or stockroom and lay a picture of it on his desk for quick observation as to just how it stands and to provide an invaluable record for reference when a requisition is placed before him for new materials or stock. A glance at the chart covering the stock on hand of a particular kind of material will verify the necessity for placing the order for the quantity covered by the requisition, or may show that the additional material is not required.

Chart No. 31 shows a weekly stock record of copper stock at a manufacturing plant, the solid line representing the stock on hand, the broken line representing the quantity used, and the vertical bars showing the quantity due on order. The difference in the height of the bar line vertically and the level of the line showing consumption represents each week the fluctuation in the line representing the stock on hand. For example, this chart, in the first week, shows 77,100 lbs. on hand (solid line), and 50,000 lbs. on order (vertical bar line) ; the second week shows 20,000 lbs. consumed (broken line), 10,500 still

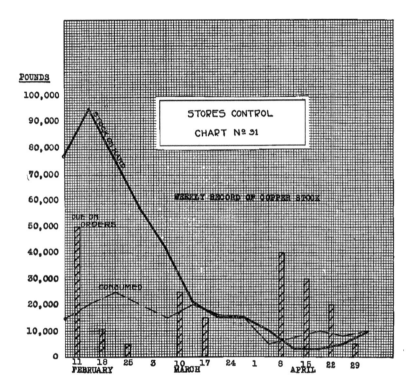

due on order (vertical bar line), and 96,100 lbs. on hand (solid line). This indicates that of the 50,000 lbs. which was due on order the previous week, 39,500 was received, as there remained due, only 10,500 lbs. As 20,500 lbs. have been consumed, the receipts have exceeded the amount consumed by 19,000, which added to the previous week's record of quantity on hand, 77,100 lbs., gives present stock on hand 96,100 lbs. You will note that the line showing quantity consumed shows a higher level on the chart in the second week, to the extent of twenty and one-half of the small blocks on the chart; that the vertical bar line has shortened thirty-nine and one-half blocks, and that the difference between these two is 19 of the small blocks. The line representing stock on hand has therefore gone up the same number of these blocks, 19, and you will see by consulting the chart that this is the case.

Having this complete information available places the executive in the enviable position of passing final judgment on material requirements, with full conviction of correctness consequent upon having in hand this definite information on which to make decisions with a minimum of effort, and practically at a glance.

There comes to mind an experience with one of the large corporations of the country which used tin-plate in packing their product. While the tin-plate did not enter directly into the product, but only into the containers, it was quite as important to them as the product itself, which latter, though it could be made could not be moved out of the plant without the tin-plate containers. This corporation was carrying an average stock of tin-plate worth about $300,000 and they were using about $20,000 worth of it per month. This stock consisted of many different sizes of tin-plate, purchased with a view to using each of the sizes to manufacture a specific kind and type of tin container, but because of lack of method, a considerable stock of odd sizes had crept in, as well as considerable stock of sizes which were little used. From the figures given, i e., $20,000 of tin-plate consumed each month, and a stock on hand averaging $300,000, it will be seen that the stock on hand was sufficient in money value to meet requirements for more than a year. The proportion of the different sizes was not correct, however, for a year's production, and, in addition, there were, as stated, many odd sizes which were not adaptable to the manufacture of any size of container except at a considerable disadvantage in waste. To remedy this situation, a chart, No. 31A, was made up of rectangles, showing each of the sizes of tinplate along the left-hand margin of the chart, and each of the kinds of containers along the top margin, a column for each container.

CHART USED TO CONTROL PURCHASES OF TIN PLATE

SIZE OF TIN PLATE	WEIGHT	REQUIREMENTS TO MAKE 1,000 COMPLETE TINS ---- BODIES,TOPS and BOTTOMS							
		#1 Tins	#2 Tins	#3 Tins	#4 Tins	#5 Tins	#6 Tins	#7 Tins	#8 Tins
18"x 16"		5 Boxes (Bodies)				6 Boxes (Bodies)			3 Boxes (Tops)
14"x 10"		2½ Boxes (Tops)	2½ Boxes (Tops)		7 Boxes (Bodies)		6 Boxes (Bodies)		
20"x 14"		2½ Boxes (Bottoms)	2½ Boxes (Bottoms)	5½ Boxes (Bodies)			2 Boxes (Tops)		7 Boxes (Bodies)
17"x 15"				2 Boxes (Tops)		4 Boxes (Tops)		6 Boxes (Bodies)	
14"x 12"				2 Boxes (Bottoms)	3 Boxes (Bottoms)		3 Boxes (Bottoms)		
16"x 14"					2 Boxes (Tops)			3 Boxes (Tops)	3 Boxes (Bottoms)
19"x 16"			5 Boxes (Bodies)			3 Boxes (Bottoms)		2½ Boxes (Bottoms)	

CHART NO 31A

In the rectangle formed by the vertical and horizontal lines is shown the number of boxes of tin-plate required to produce 1000 containers of the kind listed at the top of each column of rectangles, viz: No. 1 container is shown as requiring tin-plate 18"x16" for bodies, 14"x10" for tops, and 20"x14" for bottoms. You will note from the chart that it requires 5 boxes of 18"x16", 2½ boxes of 14"x10", and 2½ boxes of 20″x14″ tin-plate to produce 1000 of each of the parts required and therefore, 1,000 complete containers of this size.

Thus the guess-work was removed from this factor of the business by the application of this simple chart, and the corporation was enabled to operate to much better advantage financially and physically. Within 18 months after the inception of this plan, which time was required for working off much of the excess and slow-moving tin-plate, this company was operating on an average inventory of tin-plate approximating $75,000, which was about one-fourth of the average inventory of $300,000 previously carried. This meant the release or liquidating of more than $200,000 of stock, representing a considerable item even to a large corporation. This we believe illustrates something of the potentiality of charts to simplify business problems which without the charts are somewhat complex. One of the important points in this particular chart is that where two or three or even more containers are manufactured from the same size of tin-plate, a glance along the horizontal line on which any size of tin-plate is listed gives the full information of the extent to which any size of tin-plate is used, while a glance down any vertical column of rectangles tells at once just what sizes of tin-plate are used for the specific size of container listed at the top of the rectangle, and also how much of each size is required to manufacture 1,000 containers. The chart corresponds to a formula in which the ingredients have been measured by established standards, and, once done, may be used rapidly and accurately for all future cases.

CHAPTER V

BUDGET CONTROL CHARTS

Budget Control Charts—Only recently have the terms "budget" and "budget control" become common in business organizations, and it appears that increasing interest is being shown in this phase of management. The idea back of budgets is not new, for as early as 1760 the Chancellor of the Exchequer of the British Government was said to "open his budget."

Municipalities and governmental units have for a long time applied budgetary control and many people still think of budgetary control as applying only to governmental organizations. Up to June, 1921, practically all of the literature on the subject was confined to city, state or national budgets.

For many years, business organizations have estimated in advance the probable volume of business, costs and operating profit, but only recently has this been attempted in budgetary form. Few users of budgets have failed to realize their importance and usefulness. This means of forecasting the course of a business with some degree of accuracy by analysis of past performances and consideration of possibilities has been one of the greatest developments of the scientific study of business during the last twenty years. An organization guided by a well developed and comparatively accurate budget has a marked advantage over one not so guided, especially under the difficult conditions of the past few years.

Usually one official is appointed to have general control and supervision of budget estimates. This may be the Comptroller, Treasurer, or special assistant to the President. He receives from the various operating officials the estimates prepared embracing Sales, Cost of Sales, expenses, production and perhaps the estimated cash receipts and expenditures.

These estimates must be prepared with due consideration for the inter-relation of the various activities and with utmost consideration of the factors affecting them, as the executive responsible for the budget prepares his statement from them. Necessarily he must depend upon subordinates for accuracy as it would be impossible and impracticable to check every detail.

After these estimates are worked into a final statement they are submitted to the president, or chief executive, who must consider the operating programme as a whole and the resulting financial position which said programme will produce IF the estimates are realized. He sees what will result if the estimates are correct and must ascertain the probability of these results by convincing himself as to the accuracy of the estimates. Failure to attain these estimates means embarrassment, and is often caused by a lack of co-ordination between the executives responsible for sales and production (or purchases) or from insufficient control of expenditures. It is necessary that the chief executive be familiar with all conditions relating thereto in order that he appraise the budget definitely and accurately.

These estimates can not be made to exact accuracy and must be used with judgment, not arbitrarily. They are frequently influenced by personal bias and often represent what is desired rather than what may be expected.

Therefore a check upon these estimates must be made by the chief executive, which will enable him without extraordinary effort not only to satisfy himself of their soundness, but to see exactly the worst condition he may expect.

He should know before the period starts exactly the sales volume necessary to meet all costs and expenses and, at all times, whether or not the volume of business meets the estimates and is sufficient to meet current expenses. Conservatism demands that he know the maximum and minimum volume possibilities of his business.- This will give an invaluable control from which to determine facts, instead of relying upon individual opinions.

It is acknowledged that scientifically arranged budgets have not yet come into general use. Even though the government of our nation has adopted the budget plan as the most effective means of handling the finances of the country, the commercial and industrial enterprises have been slow to fall in line and should unquestionably adopt every available means of budgetary control.

Executives may not readily approve a movement no matter how good it may be, if in their minds it is likely to introduce seemingly great mental effort. Some have an inherent suspicion that modern scientific methods can not be sound simply because they have not been generally adopted.

A broad conception of the method of visualizing the budget and a realization of the benefits it offers the business executive can not fail to promote a clearer understanding of its value. Many hard-headed, practical business men will say it is too academic, impractical and complicated, when in reality it is comparatively simple and requires no great mental effort to realize its full meaning.

Ordinarily an executive will scrutinize a request for an expenditure with much concern before approving it, but the same man will approve a budget estimate of income that represents the production and purchase schedules

BUDGET OF INCOME FOR TWELVE MONTHS 1923

DATED DECEMBER 1, 1922

	**Consolidated Total	Dept. A	Dept. B	Dept. C	Dept. D	Dept. E
Total Sales	177 740	83 079	15 000	67 361	1 000	14 000
Cost of Sales	125 434	60 009	9 150	47 913	780	10 583
GROSS PROFIT ON SALES	52 306	23 070	5 850	19 448	220	3 417
Cash Discount on Sales	3 756	1 208	135	2 235	3	175
Selling Expenses	27 526	12 701	1 115	10 506	17	1 938
TOTAL DEDUCTIONS	31 282	13 909	1 250	12 741	20	2 113
Net Profit on Sales	21 023	9 161	4 600	6 707	200	1 304
Administration Expenses	5 014	2 124	600	2 152	0	138
NET OPERATING PROFIT	16 009	7 037	4 000	4 555	200	1 166
*Corporate Requirement	14 000	6 154	3 497	3 983	174	1 008
SURPLUS FOR THE PERIOD	2 009	883	503	572	26	159

* The $14,000 Corporate Requirement is distributed on the percentage of Net Operating Profits.
** Consolidated Total items do not include inter-department sales which are included in the figures of the Departments A to E.

and is virtually a request for an appropriation covering unitemized expenses, largely because of pressure of current matters, or because he can not verify the estimates and is compelled to depend entirely upon his subordinates.

It is not the object in this chapter to present at length how a budget is prepared and handled. It is rather to present a means of checking the budget and from it develop a danger point above which sales must be maintained. This gives an all-important business control without elaborate machinery and without adding to the cost of the accounting department.

For this purpose the accompanying charts have been constructed and by means of them not only is the executive enabled to determine the degree of accuracy of the estimates, but they serve also as a constant check on the actual and estimated results. This is particularly valuable as to the income estimate, which is the backbone of the budget.

These charts not only enable an executive to determine the soundness of the budget before approving it, but they offer a perpetual comparison between estimated, actual and required results.

The minimum sales requirement chart, No. 33, is constructed from the sample "Budget of Operating Income" shown on page 102, and gives the graphical, analytical and mathematical analysis of the component parts of the Budget of Operating Income as well as determining the amount of sales necessary to meet all expenses, and the various costs at a given volume of sales.

Various titles are used as synonyms for the Profit and Loss Statement, but regardless of title they all serve the same purpose in that they summarize the net balance between Income and expense for a period.

The "Budget of Income for 12 Months 1923" is an example of what is submitted to the chief executive for approval after having been prepared by the official in charge of budget activities, and shows the estimates of sales, expenses and net income or surplus, departmentally and in total. (This principle may be applied to commodities as well as to departments.)

A summary of the elementary principles of the Income Statement will simplify the "Minimum Sales Requirement" chart.

Foremost for consideration are expenses, of which some are fixed and others are expenses that vary directly with Sales. Such items as Interest on investments, Sinking Fund requirements, Dividends and certain taxes which are not a result of, but which must be met from, the current income from Sales, are hereinafter referred to as Corporate Requirements because they result directly from corporate activities.

The balance of the expenses consisting of Cost of Sales, Cash Discount on Sales, Selling Expenses, Administrative Expenses, are directly dependent upon Sales and vary accordingly; consequently they are referred to as variable expenses.

The Budget of Income shows $14,000 Corporate Requirements and $161,731 variable expenses, totaling $175,731 which, deducted from the estimated sales of $177,-740, leaves the estimated surplus or net income of $2,009.

It is to be expected that the estimates of variable expense and Sales will not be realized and with the budget as a base we will proceed to determine exactly what sales must be attained in order to meet the corporate and variable expenses as well as to determine the variable expenses at this volume of Sales. This gives a Minimum Sales, and a Maximum expense figure.

In view of the fact that the Corporate Requirements are independent of Sales and must be considered regardless of whether sales continue or not, they are given foremost consideration and are represented by the line A-B plotted at the point of $14,000 on the left-hand scale. The next item, Cost of Sales, is plotted upward from the line A-B at B to the point $139,434 (which represents $14,000 plus $125,434=$139,434). These costs vary directly in proportion to sales and are added to the corporate requirements. This relationship is shown by the line A-C.

Added to the aforementioned expenses at the point C are

1. Administration Exp.............$ 5,014	represented by the line A-D
2. Selling Expenses 27,526	represented by the line A-E
3. Cash Disc. on Sales 3,756	represented by the line A-F

$36,297

Plus
Corporate Requirements........ 14,000
Cost of Sales 125,434

$175,731   represented by Point F

Beginning with Corporate Requirements and adding thereto the remaining expenses (Chart No. 33), the points were plotted on the heavy black line running vertically from the point 177,740 on the base or horizontal scales, as follows:

Expense	Amount	Point Plotted
Corporate Requirements	14,000	14,000........B
Cost of Sales	..125,434	139,434........C
Administration Expenses	5,014	144,448........D
Selling Expenses	27,527	171,975........E
Cash Discount on Sales	3,756	175,731........F

This left a space between the points F, the line representing the cumulation of all estimated expenses, and G representing estimated sales, equal to 2,009 on the scale.

So far we have classified our expenses as Fixed and Variable and after allocating these fixed expenses on the chart have added thereto the variable expenses and coordinated them with the estimated sales which start at zero. Thus we get the same balance of 2,009 as on the income statement, proving the accuracy of the procedure.

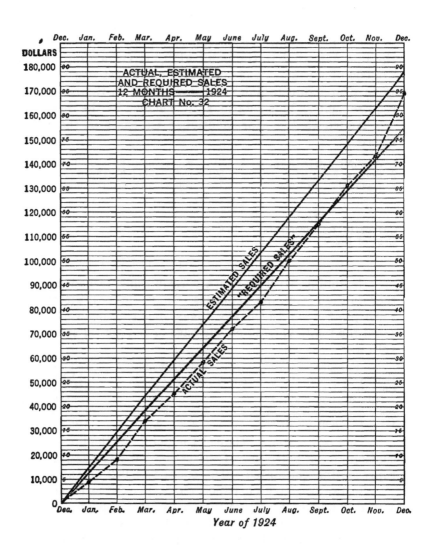

The final step is to plot the estimated sales from the point O, the intersection of the vertical and horizontal scales, to the point G, which represents $177,740 on both scales. This is represented by the red line O-G.

The point X ($155,400) at which the line OG, Estimated Sales, intersects the line OF, Total Costs, represents the amount of Sales required to meet all expenses.

These expenses are cumulated on the chart and the readings of costs may be made for any amount of sales up to and including the estimated by locating the amount of sales on either the horizontal or vertical scale and following it through to the line representing the expenses thereof. The space between the two lines represents the amount of expense for that particular element of total cost and may be ascertained by deducting the reading of the lower line on the scale at this point from the reading of the upper line.

The accuracy of this chart has been proven mathematically, and, once satisfied, an executive may substitute business terms for mathematical terms and apply the equation:

$$\text{Minimum Sales} = \frac{\text{Corporate Requirements}}{1 - \dfrac{\text{Variable Costs}}{\text{Estimated Sales}}}$$

using the estimates submitted:

$$\text{Minimum Sales} = \frac{14,000}{1 - \dfrac{161,731}{177,740}}$$

$$= \$155,382$$

The solution may be proven either graphically, by means of the chart, or mathematically, by means of the equation.

Once the required amount of sales is determined, the various expenses at this point may be determined by reading along the line X.

SALES REQUIREMENTS

ANALYSIS OF BUDGET ESTIMATE OF INCOME
AND EXPENSE TO DETERMINE THE MINIMUM
AMOUNT OF SALES NECESSARY TO MEET ALL
EXPENSES AND TO COMPARE ACTUAL AND
ESTIMATED EXPENSES
12 MONTHS 1923
CHART No. 33

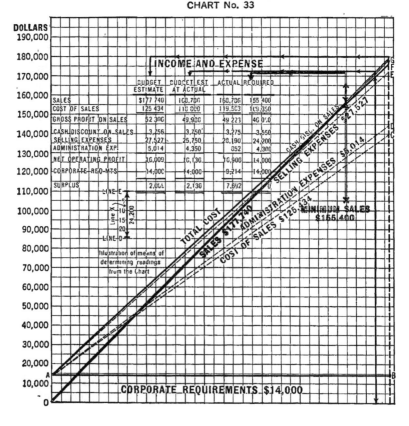

These items are shown under the column headed "Required" on the chart. This permits a check on expenses to determine which are or are not within the budget estimate.

Satisfied that the minimum Sales Requirement chart and the equation serve as a double check upon the requirements, the executive need only plot the estimated and required sales as shown on Chart No. 32, inserting from month to month the actual sales as reported. Thus he knows exactly whether—

1. Actual Sales are sufficient to meet all expenses

2. "   " exceed or are less than the estimated, sufficiently well in advance to further determine exactly where the responsibility lies in the event of a large difference between actual and estimated results.

It is obvious from Chart No. 32 that for the first nine months, Sales were insufficient to meet all requirements and at no time during the twelve months did the actual Sales exceed the estimated. Something evidently was amiss in the estimates and it now remains to determine what items varied from the estimate and to what degree.

This was accomplished by means of the statement on the following page. The expense items were read from the chart at the point of $168,786, the twelve months actual sales, and represent the budget estimates at this volume as shown on the chart.

An analysis of the statement shows the following interesting facts:

1. Administration expenses were over-estimated $3,498, over 400%.

2. The Corporate Requirements were overestimated by $4,786 (approximately 52%).

3. Selling expenses were much too large in comparison with the estimates and practically accounted for the difference between the estimated and actual net

COMPARISON OF ACTUAL, ESTIMATED AND REQUIRED
SALES WITH READINGS FROM THE SALES REQUIREMENT
CHART AT ACTUAL SALES $168,786.00

	Budget Estimate	Required	Actual	%	Reading from Chart at $168,786 Sales	%	Diff. between actual and readings from chart Dollars
Total Sales	177 740	155 400	168 786	100.	168 786	100.	
Cost of Sales	125 434	109 350	119 563	70.837	118 800	70.384	763.
Gross Profit on Sales	52 306	46 050	49 223	29.162	49 986	29.615	—763.
Cash Discount on Sales	3 756	3 550	3 275	1.940	3 750	2.221	—475.
Selling Expenses	27 526	24 200	28 190	16.701	25 750	15.255	2 440.
Total Deductions	31 282	27 750	31 465	18.641	29 500	17.476	1 965.
Net Profit on Sales	21 023	18 300	17 758	10.520	20 486	12.139	—2 728.
Administration Expenses	5 014 *1*	4 300 *1*	852 *1*	.504 *1*	4 350 *1*	2.576	—3 498. *1*
Net Operating Profit	16 009	14 000	16 906	10.016	16 136	9.563	770.
Corporate Requirements	14 000 *2*	14 000	9 214 *2*	5.458	14 000 *2*	8.294	—4 786. *2*
Surplus for the Period	2 009	0	7 692 *3*	4.558	2 136	1.269	5 556.

Surplus shown on chart................................ 2 136
Variations from Estimate:
Over-estimate of Cash Discount *1* 475
  " " Admin. Exp. *1* 3 498
  " " Corporate Req. *2* 4 786

What Surplus should have been........ 10 895
Actual Surplus *3* 7 692

Difference 3 203
Accounted for by Excess of Actual:
Over-estimated:
  Cost of Sales 763
  Selling Expenses ... 2 440
                           3 203
                           3 203

Operating Profit.

4. Cost of Sales exceeded the estimate by $763.

5. Cash Discounts on Sales were less than the estimates.

Thus the executive is enabled to measure the accuracy of the estimates and see the weak points which otherwise would escape his attention.

Having a means of accurately checking the Budget of Income, the executive next concerns himself with the physical measurement and programme of production (or purchases) estimated to meet the anticipated demands, bearing in mind at all times the capital tied up in inventory and the resulting turnover thereof.

It is necessary therefore that an analysis be made of the production programme, co-ordinating it with the original inventory and estimated Sales.

No special business or mathematical training is necessary to comprehend that the Inventory at the beginning of the month plus the scheduled Production for the month less the estimated Sales for that month represents the estimated inventory at the beginning of the ensuing month. By repeating this for the twelve months, the estimated inventory with which the year will end is readily ascertained.

To a great majority this may appear elementary, but what percentage of the readers of this book could take the following inventory as of the beginning of the year, production schedule and sales estimates monthly, and, after the closest consideration, conscientiously say that the mental impression registered is as sharp as that from the accompanying charts, Nos. 34 and 35?

They clearly visualize the conditions planned, and co-ordinate these factors in a simple and effective way, showing the estimated sales and production so as to prevent over-production and the resulting excessive inventory.

These charts represent units but it is comparatively

BUDGET ESTIMATE OF SALES, PRODUCTION
AND
INVENTORIES AS OF THE 1ST OF THE MONTH

	Budget Estimated Sales (Units)		Production Schedule (Units)		Estimated Inventory (Units)	
Jan.	133		199		*258	(Actual)
Feb.	146		191		324	
2 Mos.		280		390		
Mar.	208		223		369	
3 Mos.		488		614		
Apr.	167		234		384	
4 Mos.		656		848		
May	171		216		450	
5 Mos.		827		1,065		
June	165		192		496	
6 Mos.		992		1,257		
July	190		168		523	
7 Mos.		1,183		1,425		
Aug.	233		220		500	
8 Mos.		1,417		1,646		
Sept.	222		184		488	
9 Mos.		1,639		1,830		
Oct.	224		223		450	
10 Mos.		1,864		2,053		
Nov.	182		223		448	
11 Mos.		2,046		2,277		
Dec.	279		164		488	
12 Mos.		2,326		2,441		
Jan. 1st, 1924					373	

easy to substitute monetary values, in which case Sales
must be figured at cost.

Besides serving to determine the advisability of the
production programme submitted, these charts may be
corrected at the end of each month by inserting the actual
Production, Sales, and resulting Inventory thereby giving
a perpetual comparison between estimated and actual results, and serving as a danger signal when estimates are
inaccurate.

They show this very clearly and concisely. In this
specific case it had been desirable to turn over the January 1st inventory 10 times per year and as result of a

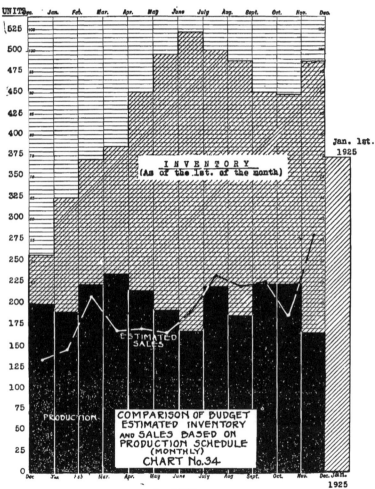

COMPARISON OF BUDGET
ESTIMATED INVENTORY
AND SALES BASED ON
PRODUCTION SCHEDULE
(MONTHLY)
CHART No.34

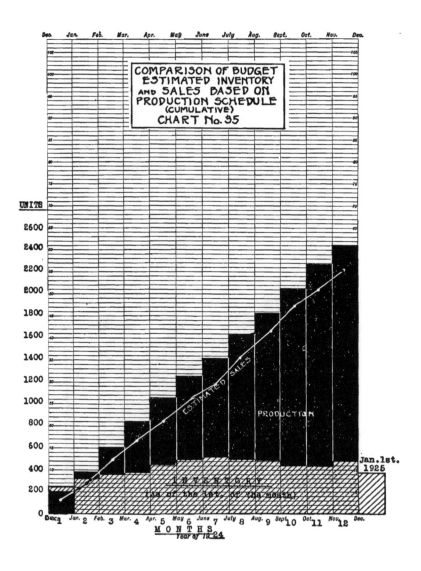

COMPARISON OF BUDGET
ESTIMATED INVENTORY
AND SALES BASED ON
PRODUCTION SCHEDULE
(CUMULATIVE)
CHART No. 35

thorough analysis of Sales activities it was shown that 260 units were sufficient inventory with which to start the year. Therefore it was desirable to arrange the production programme accordingly.

However, upon visualizing the Budget Estimate it showed that the production programme averaged about 200 units per month indicating neither a marked increase nor decrease throughout the year; that the Sales were on the upward trend through the year; and that the inventory showed a very decided increase for the first seven months of the year, being somewhat reduced in August, September, October and November by the excess of estimated Sales over production during that period.

With the production programme submitted, which exceeds the estimated sales for eight months of the year, it is only natural that the closing inventory will be much larger than desired. This may be considered the worst possible condition, for, should the December estimated sales fail to be realized the Inventory condition would be much worse.

The chart further shows a continuous increase in Inventory as the result of an excess of production over sales for the first six months.

Further observation fails to indicate sufficient increase in estimated sales during the remainder of the year to warrant the scheduled production for the first half.

A consideration of the cumulative Sales and production (Chart No. 35) further convinces of the exaggerated production schedule wherein the production, without considering the original inventory, exceeds the estimated sales for the last 11 months.

Realizing that the average executive loses much of the relation of the elements of his budget because of their magnitude the object of these charts is to bring them into a small form and to make these elements clearer and easier to see and comprehend. They enable him to keep his finger on the pulse of that very important phase of business, the budget.

A little patience, concentration, and an application of the ordinary principles of common sense are all that is required to fully comprehend their utmost meaning and value.

CHAPTER VI

ROUTINE CHARTS

The usefulness of routine charts in an organization is unlimited. They lessen the labor of interpreting in- structions and reports that are ordinarily presented in lengthy typewritten reports, and immediately reveal dupli- cations, inconsistencies, and unnecessary work. They also serve as a basis for improvements in routine methods.

Mr. G. Charter Harrison is the exponent of this work and its progress is largely due to his efforts. His charts cover all of the routine operations incidental to production methods.

In the issue for April, 1923, of MANAGEMENT EN- GINEERING, Mr. Harrison had an article under the caption

The Use of Routine Charts
In Improving and Systematizing Office Procedure

from which the following excerpts are taken

"Some time ago the writer (Mr. Harrison) was pres- ent at a discussion which occurred in the office of the presi- dent of a large manufacturing concern. A question was raised as to what safeguards were in force to insure the accuracy of the piece-work pay-roll. The comptroller, who was present, was exceedingly vague on the subject, but suggested that as the cost accountant was entirely familiar with the details of the pay-roll he should there- fore be able to answer the question satisfactorily. The cost accountant was accordingly sent for, but he, too,

117

proved to have exceedingly sketchy ideas on the subject. Of one thing, however, he was certain, and that was that the paymaster would be able to give the information required. Enter the paymaster, who denied emphatically that the question was one which he should be called upon to answer, as the preparation and checking of the piece-work pay-roll was a duty of the chief factory clerk. Here the investigation was temporarily blocked, as the chief factory clerk was at home sick, so the president, who by this time was getting hot under the collar, went out in the shop to get the information himself. But even this drastic action did not produce the results as rapidly as might have been expected, for it developed that there was no fixed routine in the matter, each shop clerk, with true American individuality, following that particular line of procedure he thought the best.

"**Difficulties Involved in Improving Routine** —Altogether, it was an illuminating experience and typical of that vagueness which so often exists as to clerical routine.

"That such a condition should exist is not so astonishing when one considers that the time of the average minor executive is generally too much taken up with the immediate business in hand to give much thought to the devising of ways and means for improving the routine of his department. Furthermore, if he should prove to be ambitious, his field of action is limited, for however closely his work may be related to that of other departments any attempt on his part to investigate the methods of these departments is apt to be regarded as an intrusion and so resented.

"One reason why the expert called in from the outside is often able to obtain remarkable results is because he is not subjected to the handicaps mentioned above. He is not constantly called away by the demands of the day's routine and is accordingly able to concentrate on the problem in hand. Furthermore, it is understood that it is distinctly within his province to investigate the affairs of all departments, and he is therefore not harassed by interdepartmental suspicions and jealousies.

"Flexible Experience of Outside Adviser—The outside adviser, of course, possesses other advantages. To start with, he has made a special study of this particular class of work, and in this, as in other things, practice tends to make perfect. His angle of vision has been broadened by the constant interchange of ideas with numerous executives in many lines of business, so that he should be able to bring to bear on the problems to be solved, not only his own ideas and experience, but also those of other men of ability. For these reasons, therefore, there will probably always be a demand for the services of the trained investigator, but nevertheless there is a great deal of useful work which can be accomplished without the aid of outside professional assistance, and the purpose of this article is to offer some constructive suggestions, based upon the writer's personal experience, as to the best way in which to approach the problem of increasing the efficiency of routine clerical work.

"It is axiomatic, of course, that the first step toward improving present methods is to obtain a very complete and clear understanding of what these methods are, and yet the writer is constantly coming across instances where changes have been made in routine methods which have resulted disastrously, all because the originator of the changes did not have a clear understanding of the routine he was revolutionizing. In system work, nothing will take the place of clear thinking—all the Coué philosophy in the world will not make a poorly designed plan function satisfactorily, and instead of "every day in every way becoming better and better," the situation will be more nearly like that described by Edmund Spenser:

And being once amisse growes daily wourse and wourse.

To obtain a complete understanding of the clerical routine of a large business is naturally a proposition of considerable magnitude. Happily, however, one does not have to cover the whole ground at once, and the first step to be taken is to map out the work in sections and then to take up one section at a time. Suggestions as to some of the divisions which would probably be made are as fol-. lows:

Routine in connection with the handling of a customer's order from its receipt in the mail up to the shipping and billing of the goods

Routine in connection with purchasing material

Routine in connection with the pay-roll

Disbursements routine

Traffic department routine

General accounting routine

Cost department routine, etc., etc.

"**Procedure of the Inexperienced**—Now the usual procedure followed by the inexperienced in these matters is to obtain copies of all forms used, on which he makes elaborate notes, and then to prepare a typewritten report in which he describes the routine in detail and makes suggestions as to its improvement. If the work is done at all thoroughly, this report is a voluminous affair, is about as interesting reading as a railroad time-table, and takes as long to understand as it did to prepare. Generally the executive who is called upon to pass on the suggestions made refuses to be bothered with the task of partaking of and digesting so uninviting a repast. When one considers the vast array of machinery which has been designed for the purpose of saving the time of the man at the bench, one sometimes wonders that so little has been done in connection with the saving of the time of executives. How much of the time of the average busy executive is wasted

in studying voluminous, detailed and indigestible accounting reports and in passing on half-baked ideas? It might
be suggested that in place of that common and idiotic
motto, "Do it now" (which policy too often results in has-
ty, unconsidered action, and in "doing it wrong"), the following biblical quotation be prominently displayed in the
executive's office:

Write the vision, and make it plain upon tables, that he that runs
may read.

"That very remarkable man, the late John H. Patterson, was a strong advocate of what he called "teaching by
the eye," so much so that he even referred to it in his
will in the following words: "I am also a great believer
in the great efficiency of teaching by the eye, and I here-
by commend that branch of educational work." Mr.
Patterson realized very fully that in order to be able to
understand a subject thoroughly it is necessary to obtain
a clear picture of it. Francis Bacon once said that "truth
will emerge sooner from error than confusion," and the
first step in the solution of any problem is to see it clearly.
Now there is no man living who can carry in his mind a
clear picture of the multitudinous interrelated motions
involved in the conduct of a large modern business, where
the number of forms used will run into four figures and
where the number of routine operations will aggregate
many thousands. And assuming that such a person did
exist, without the aid of concrete illustrations he could
not convey the picture in his own mind to that of others.

"An Example of Ordering Material Routine—In Chart
No. 36 is shown a practical illustration of a picture or
routine chart of the method followed by a concern in
handling one section of its work, namely, the ordering of
material to meet the requirements of its manufacturing
schedules. There is nothing remarkable about this routine chart, but it does give us what we want, namely, a
clear-cut, definite understanding of what is being done.

Furthermore, it places us in a position to give anyone else an equally clear idea, and this at a minimum expenditure of time.

"Mention has previously been made of the difficulty experienced by the head of a department introducing new ideas owing to the distaste of one department head to having the head of another department investigate his methods. It is impossible, however, to consider routine methods solely from the standpoint of a single department—all business activities are so closely inter-related that to organize them in such a manner as to eliminate all wasted effort and duplication of work it is essential that the routine should be considered as a whole and in the interest of the business generally, instead of from the standpoint of the convenience and efficiency of individual departments.

"It is generally and very properly considered, however, that it is the duty of the comptroller of a corporation to act as a co-ordinating and harmonizing factor in connection with the improvement of routine methods. He, therefore, is the logical person to supervise and direct all work done along the line of introducing improvements and refinements in clerical work not only in the office but also in the factory.

"A wise comptroller will not try to force his ideas on his business associates. It is essential that he should sell them. Changes in methods are always more or less troublesome, and obviously a department head has got to be pretty thoroughly convinced that the proposed change is a mighty good thing before he becomes enthusiastic about it. It is therefore strictly up to the comptroller properly to present his plans—to give clear pictures of both the present and proposed methods so that the advantages which may be expected from the adoption of the latter stand out clearly and unmistakably. No diffi-

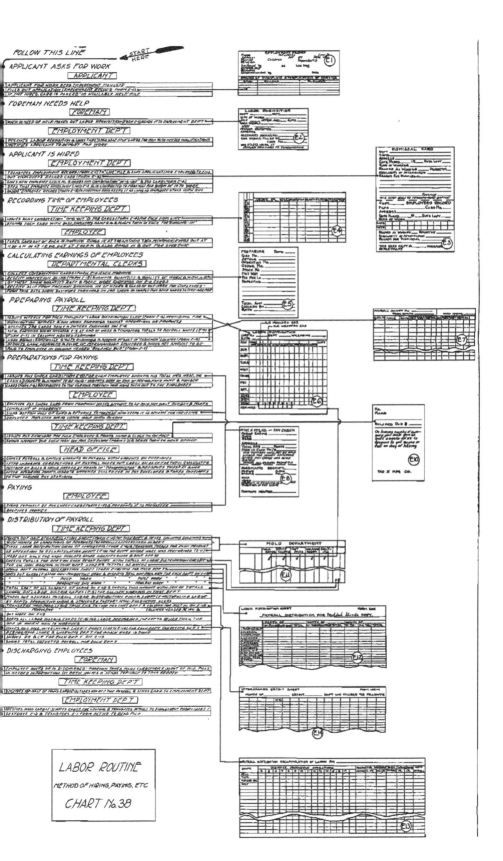

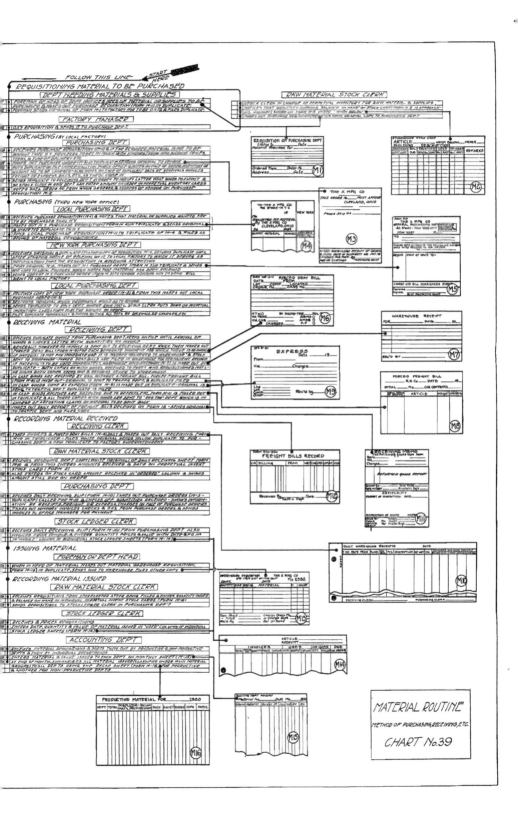

MATERIAL ROUTINE

METHOD OF PURCHASING & RECEIVING, ETC.

CHART No. 39

culty will ever be experienced in getting support in introducing a really desirable improvement, and the routine charts give the comptroller a simple and effective means of demonstrating that his proposed changes are worth while. And if the charts do not clearly show that the pros more than offset the cons, then the comptroller is spared from placing himself in the embarrassing position of recommending changes which are not advisable."

As a further illustration of what can be done to tie the facts and details of a routine into a connected picture, we are submitting the accompanying Labor Routine Chart and Material Routine Chart which were developed for one of our largest manufacturing organizations.

It is obvious that it would require many pages to put these systems in written form, but when visualized by means of a chart they are shown so that all detail and inter-relation is before the eye at one and the same time. The manner in which individual functions, forms and procedures are associated with one another and with the whole becomes readily apparent.

The text on the left-hand side includes all necessary information and at the same time correlates all forms and figures. The greatest value of these charts to the executive is in the fact that they reduce the process of mental visualization to a minimum. Should he desire some information about the way his payroll is distributed or material handled, which he would ordinarily get only by reading and digesting a lengthy written statement, he sees practically at a glance with very little effort the relation between the functions, the duties of individuals, and the forms and figures involved. This inter-relation is visualized physically, thus relieving the executive of a mental effort that is both ineffectual and fatiguing.

The chart also assists in the matter of supervision. To properly supervise, it is necessary to know not only

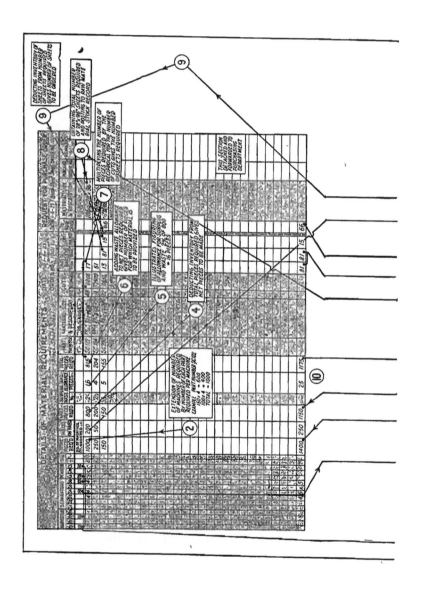

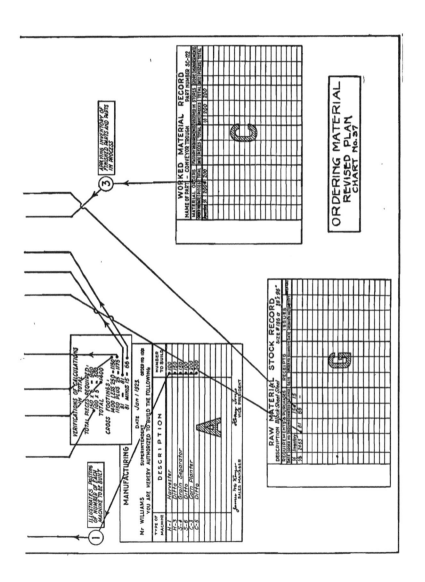

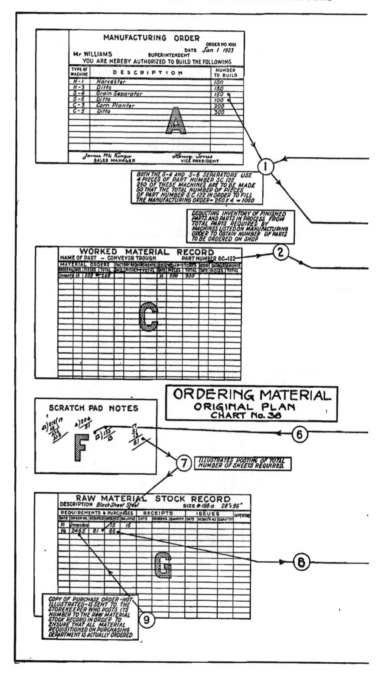

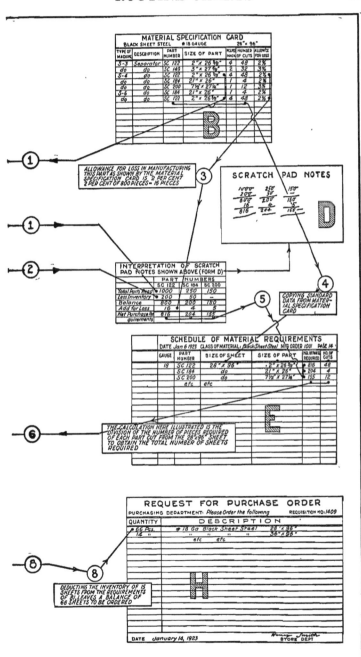

MATERIAL SPECIFICATION CARD

BLACK SHEET STEEL　＃18 GAUGE　28"× 96"

TYPE OF MACHINE	DESCRIPTION	PART NUMBER	SIZE OF PART	MICRO MACH	NUMBER OF CUTS	ALLOWED FOR LOSS
S-3	Separator	SC 122	2"× 26 1/8"	4	48	2%
do	do	SC 149	3"× 27 5/8"	2	32	3%
S-4	do	SC 122	2"× 26 1/8"	4	48	2%
do	do	SC 184	21"× 26"	1	4	2%
do	do	SC 200	7 1/2"× 27 1/4"	1	12	3%
S-6	do	SC 184	21"× 26"	1	4	2%
do	do	SC 122	2"× 26 1/8"	4	48	2%

B

ALLOWANCE FOR LOSS IN MANUFACTURING
THIS PART AS SHOWN BY THE MATERIAL
SPECIFICATION CARD IS 2 PER CENT
2 PER CENT OF 800 PIECES = 16 PIECES

SCRATCH PAD NOTES

D

**INTERPRETATION OF SCRATCH
PAD NOTES SHOWN ABOVE (FORM D)**

	PART NUMBERS		
	SC 122	SC 184	SC 200
Total Parts Req'd	1000	250	150
Less Inventory	200	50	—
Balance	800	200	150
Add for Loss	16	4	5
Net Purchase Requirements	816	204	155

COPYING STANDARD
DATA FROM MATER-
IAL SPECIFICATION
CARD

SCHEDULE OF MATERIAL REQUIREMENTS

DATE Jan 6 1923　CLASS OF MATERIAL: Black Sheet Steel　MFG ORDER 1001　PAGE 14

GAUGE	PART NUMBER	SIZE OF SHEET	SIZE OF PART	NO. OF PARTS REQUIRED	NO. OF CUTS
18	SC 122	28"× 96"	2"× 26 1/8"	816	48
	SC 184	do	21"× 26"	204	4
	SC 200	do	7 1/2"× 27 1/4"	155	12
	etc	etc			

E

THE CALCULATION HERE ILLUSTRATED IS THE
DIVISION OF THE NUMBER OF PIECES REQUIRED
OF EACH PART CUT FROM THE 28"×96" SHEET
TO OBTAIN THE TOTAL NUMBER OF SHEETS
REQUIRED

REQUEST FOR PURCHASE ORDER

PURCHASING DEPARTMENT: Please Order the following　REQUISITION NO. 1409

QUANTITY	DESCRIPTION
66 Pcs.	＃18 Ga Black Sheet Steel　28"× 96"
14 "	"　"　"　"　36"× 96"
	etc　etc

H

DEDUCTING THE INVENTORY OF 15
SHEETS FROM THE REQUIREMENTS
OF 81 LEAVES A BALANCE OF
66 SHEETS TO BE ORDERED

DATE　January 16, 1923　Henry Smith　STORE DEPT

each part of the system, but also the system in its entirety. The whole administrative method of handling labor is shown on one chart, likewise the method of handling material, giving the executive a bird's-eye view of each.

Each chart shows the procedure as it exists. With these charts in front of him, the executive can readily pick out weak spots, decide on changes and outline them on the chart as would an engineer bluepencil his changes on a print. He can change the forms, re-arrange the departmental function, arrange differently for transfer of figures, etc., in such a way that he knows what these changes will mean to each part of the system and avoid making decisions which, while favorable for one part of the routine, may handicap the rest.

CHART No. 40 FACTORY ORDER ROUTINE	ORDER DEPT	FACTORY FOREMAN	SHIPPING DEPT	COST DEPT	BILLING DEPT
Issues Factory Order in triplicate					
Puts down Official No of article ordered					
Receives copy					
Puts down quantity in stock					
Shows quantity to be made					
Hands original to workman					
Puts down weights					
Sends completed goods with Orig to Ship Dept					
Receives goods and orig and compares with duplic					
Shows number of boxes, crates, fin wt etc					
Receives copy					
Transfers all information from Orig to Triplic					
Files copy					
Makes out invoice from original					

CHART NO. 40

The executive can further use this chart to organize or change his personnel, assign work and give instructions. For instance, in the Timekeeping Department it is sufficient merely to inform a man that he will be responsible for duties outlined between Nos. 35 to 52 on the Labor Routine Chart. No further instructions are necessary as the duties are clearly outlined on the chart.

The more complicated the system the more necessary

it is for the benefit of all concerned that it be presented
in graphic form. The general plan of such a chart may
be varied to suit the requirements of any kind of routine.

Another form of routine chart is shown on the Factory Order Routine Chart No. 40, and illustrates the various courses taken by a factory order.

It readily shows that the Order Department has the
greatest need for using the Factory Order. Three copies
originate from this Department, and the triplicate is retained exclusively by it. The original is used by the
Order Department on five different occasions, and by the
Shipping Department on four different occasions. At the
same time, the Shipping Department uses the duplicate
on three different occasions. This indicates a repetition
of effort and recording which otherwise would never be
noticed.

CHAPTER VII

ORGANIZATION CHARTS

By charting the outline of an organization the position of each member of the organization with relation to all other members, is definitely shown. An Organization Chart is the surest, quickest and most comprehensive means of showing what the organization is, the various divisions to which each is responsible and all subordinate thereto. Industrial organization is the development of a functional structure with a definite scope of activities for each individual or group of individuals therein.

Organization Charts serve a useful purpose in keeping every one thinking of the co-relation of functions. Confusion will be avoided if it is remembered that they serve three distinct purposes.

1. To show the line of responsibility
2. To show the functions
3. To show how the functions are distributed

Every organization will differ somewhat from every other organization, because the objects, the results that are sought and the way these results must be obtained, are different; moreover the material out of which the organization is made differs in kind.

However, the similarity rather than the difference should be emphasized. The following skeleton chart, No. 41, of a business organization is divided into three functional zones according to the character of the functions existing in each zone.

Zone One is concerned with Policy Formation, that is, with the formulating of policies and plans, and represents the Administrative Group.

Zone Two is concerned with the Planning and establishing of an organization to carry out the policies established by the members of Zone One. This is the Management Group.

THE ZONES OF BUSINESS FUNCTIONS IN A
MANUFACTURING ORGANIZATION

ZONE 1	STOCKHOLDERS, DIRECTORS, PRESIDENT AND STAFF.	ADMINISTRATION CONCERNED WITH THE LONG RUN MAJOR POLICIES.
ZONE 2	MANUFACTURING EXECUTIVE SALES EXECUTIVE COMPTROLLER	MANAGEMENT CONCERNED WITH THE ORGANIZATION, FORMATION OF MINOR POLICIES AND RESPONSIBLE MANAGEMENT.
ZONE 3	FACTORY MANAGERS BRANCH MANAGERS WORKERS, CLERKS ETC.	PERFORMANCE CONCERNED WITH THE PERFORMANCE OF POLICIES OUTLINED.

CHART No. 41

Zone Three is concerned with the routine operations and is the Performance Group.

This diagram should not leave the impression that it is possible to draw a distinct line between the zones shown. Even Zone Three in Routine Operations involves responsible management and administration.

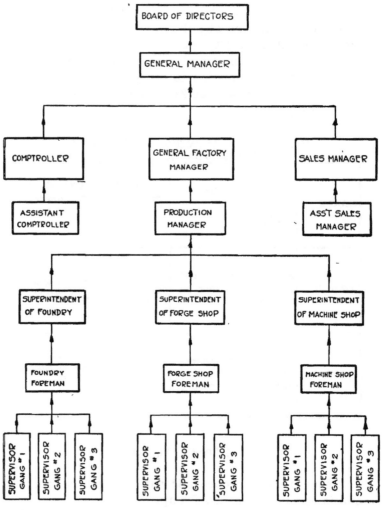

LINE TYPE OF ORGANIZATION SHOWING LINES OF RESPONSIBILITY

CHART No 42

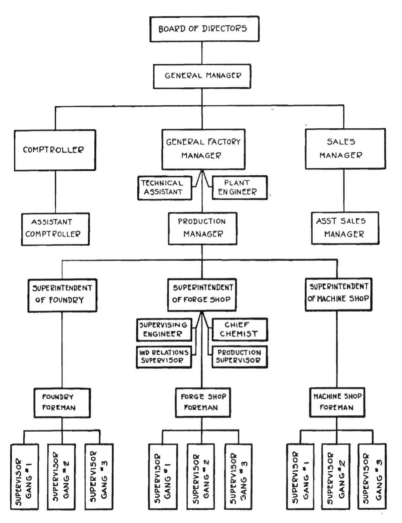

LINE & STAFF TYPE OF ORGANIZATION

CHART № 43

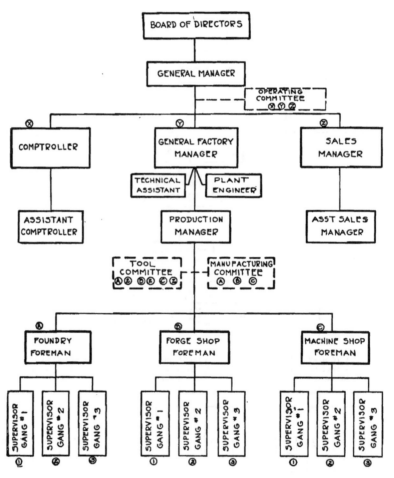

COMMITTEE TYPE OF ORGANIZATION

CHART N° 44

Each zone considered independently contains the functions of administration, management and performance.

Because of the complex character of many organizations in the various industries it is impossible to formulate fixed rules for the charting of any organization. There

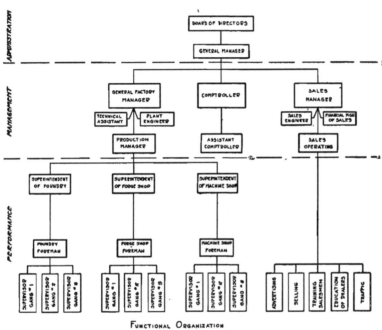

FUNCTIONAL ORGANIZATION
CHART № 45

are, however, certain types of organization that are worthy of note.

The Line Type or Military plan of organization is shown on Chart No. 42. Under this system, lines of direction and instruction are vertical, with one man at the head who deputizes duties and responsibilities to subordinates

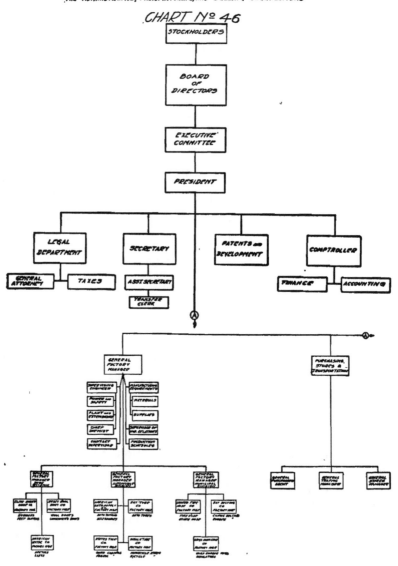

Chart Of A Large Industrial Organization Showing
The Administrative, Manufacturing, and Selling Organizations

CHART Nº 46

who are directly responsible to him. They in turn have assistants who are again held responsible for their subordinates; the matter of operating results is put up to each succeeding lower officer in the line by the officer at the top.

The Line and Staff type is shown on Chart No. 43. It is an extension of the line type in that the additional members composing the staff consist of experts and hired specialists who advise the Line Executives as to the best method for handling their organization. The staff members are not officers in any department. Each is a specialist in some phase of the Company's business and is conversant with other classes of business. It recognizes the value of specialization.

The Committee Type is shown on Chart No. 44.

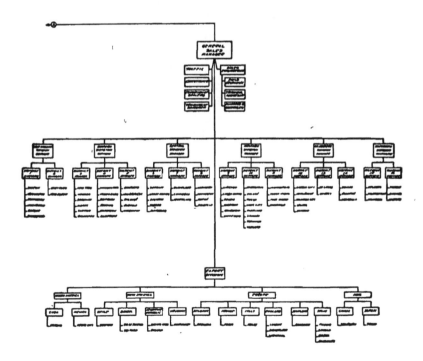

This type of organization consists of various committees who are responsible for the operating activities. Each function is represented by a committee and special committees are appointed to account and report on matters of new methods, policies, etc.

This type exemplifies "Government with the consent of the Governed.

The Function Type of organization is shown on Charts Nos. 45 and 46.

This type of organization was originated by Frederick W. Taylor and sub-divides every function of the business into its final elements, whence this analysis is given to an expert to determine how these functions may be handled more efficiently when directed toward a specific purpose by the average person so that every worker whether executive or clerk will have the fewest possible duties to perform. This form does away with the one man at the head and retains and extends the Line and Staff type of organization to include direct control of routine work. It brings expert guidance and counsel into immediate contact with the worker. Functional control must be distinguished from specialized departmentalization. It means the selection of some function of the work common to all departments and placing control of this feature in the hands of those most capable in that specific function.

With this in mind and with reference to the various sample organization charts herein it should not be difficult to outline on a chart the organization of any particular enterprise.

Various other types of organization charts have been constructed but the "box" type is simplest to construct, most widely used and as concise as any in use.

APPENDIX A

SALES QUOTAS AND SALES CONTROL

As the material in Chapter III dealing with the sales situation proved so helpful, a further development of the graphic analysis of sales is presented.

For this analysis it was decided to ascertain what were the fullest sales possibilities in each of the 48 States of the country, sales organization being national in scope. The particular product under investigation was an electric vacuum cleaner, and the maximum possibilities were considered to be a sale in each house, or rather in each building wired for electricity, since, obviously, a building not wired for electricity offered no possibility of a sale. The number of electrically wired structures in each state was available from government statistics, and these were listed as per Table I. Then the possibilities of production in the manufacturing plant were ascertained. The total structures wired throughout the entire country, by states, were found to be approximately 7,500,000, while the maximum normal production capacity of the factory supplying these machines was 6,500 per month. The waste of expense and effort in building up a sales force greater than would be required to market the entire factory output must be avoided. The production capacity of 6,500 per month, compared with the sales possibilities, showed that sales each month to one-tenth of one percent of the structures electrically wired throughout the United States would absorb the entire factory production for that month, one-tenth of one percent being the sale of one machine for

TABLE I.

State	Sales Potential	Percentage of Sales Quota	Sales Expectations
Ala.	63,683	.849	636
Ariz.	15,702	.209	157
Ark.	58,578	.781	585
Cal.	681,792	9.091	6,817
Colo.	120,438	1.606	1,204
Conn.	145,631	1.942	1,456
Del.	11,266	.150	112
Fla.	81,426	1.086	814
Ga.	98,076	1.308	980
Ida.	46,376	.618	463
Ill.	760,788	10.144	7,607
Ind.	240,268	3.204	2,402
Iowa	130,525	1.740	1,305
Kan.	177,071	2.361	1,770
Ky.	109,621	1.462	1,096
La.	54,446	.726	544
Me.	94,430	1.259	944
Md.	60,766	.810	607
Mass.	411,384	5.485	4,113
Mich.	307,424	4.099	3,074
Minn.	228,479	3.046	2.284
Miss.	43,265	.577	432
Mo.	251,570	3.354	2,515
Mont.	62,346	.831	623
Neb.	107.798	1.437	1,077
Nev.	17,598	.235	175
N. H.	36,338	.485	363
N. J.	242,953	3.239	2,429
N. M.	16,164	.216	161
N. Y.	530,979	7.080	5,309
N. C.	59,793	.797	597
N. D.	51,408	.685	514
Ohio	440,552	5.874	4,405
Okla.	83,857	1.118	838
Ore.	97,225	1.296	972
Pa.	444,198	5.923	4,441
R. I.	50,800	.677	508
S. C.	61,981	.826	619
S. D.	47,762	.637	477
Tenn.	66,235	.883	662
Tex.	265,911	3.545	2,659
Utah	83,370	1.112	833
Vt.	44,140	.589	441
Va.	11,302	.151	113
Wash.	243,063	3.241	2,430
W. Va.	45,210	.603	452
Wisc.	179,502	2.393	1,795
Wyo.	16,504	.220	165
TOTALS	7,500,994	100.000	75,000

each one thousand houses wired in the United States. Chart 1-A was therefore planned alloting a vertical bar to each state, drawn to the scale of sales potentiality or sales expectations, shown at the left-hand margin. On the right-hand margin of the chart there was placed the year's advertising-allotment scale of $5.00 per machine, thus showing at one time and in coordination, the sales expectation in each state and the advertising allowance permissible in the endeavor to realize the sales expectations. This chart sets up standards of performance, so to speak, which impress themselves on the mind of the observer so forcibly as to be memorized without mental effort.

A monthly chart, illustrated by Fig. 2-A was then laid out to show a current comparison of the sales quota (as assigned in Chart 1-A) and actual sales. In this chart, the first column shows the state, and the second column the number of machines which must be sold each month to reach the quota. Each of the next twelve columns on the chart covers a month of the year, and the top group of five rectangles, X, under each month represents the month's quota against which is to be blocked in the actual sales. Thus, the actual sales are to the full quota as the blocked in area is to the full area of the rectangles. Note that the group of rectangles for each month consists of five. These five rectangles are provided on the chart so that each month's business may thereby be readily recorded in fifths, which means that each rectangle represents twenty percent (20%) of a month's sales quota. As stated, the subdivision of this space into five rectangles is for convenience only, in recording more easily a desired fraction of one hundred percent (100%) of the sales quota. If found more convenient, four rectangles might be provided, each representing 25%; or any number of rectangles which would give the maximum of convenience.

The section Y, immediately below this group of five

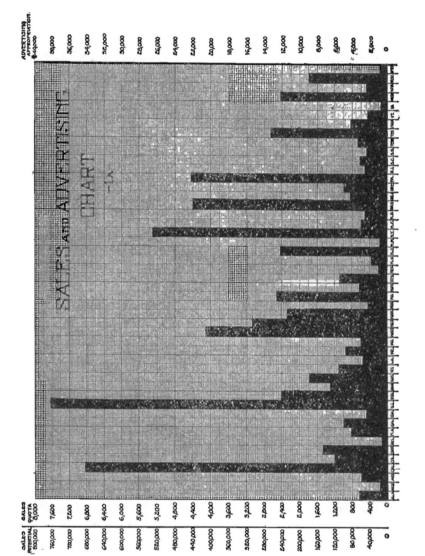

rectangles is provided for blocking out a record of sales each month in excess of the sales quota, allowing up to 100% excess. This section is also divided into five rect-angles indicating respectively 20, 40, 60, 80 and 100 per-

SALES CONTROL CHART

TERRITORY	QUOTA		YEAR 1925											
		JAN	FEB	MAR	APR	MAY	JUNE	JULY	AUG	SEPT	OCT	NOV	DEC
ALABAMA	PER MONTH – 55												
	PER YEAR – 636												
ARIZONA	PER MONTH – 13												
	PER YEAR – 157												
ARKANSAS	PER MONTH – 49												
	PER YEAR – 585												
CALIFORNIA	PER MONTH – 568												
	PER YEAR – 6,817												
COLORADO	PER MONTH – 100												
	PER YEAR – 1204												
CONNECTICUT	PER MONTH – 121												
	PER YEAR – 1,436												
DELAWARE	PER MONTH – 9												
	PER YEAR – 112												
FLORIDA	PER MONTH – 68												
	PER YEAR – 814												
GEORGIA	PER MONTH – 82												
	PER YEAR – 980												
IDAHO	PER MONTH – 39												
	PER YEAR – 463												

No. 2ᴀ

copyrighted – 1925 by N A Savage – R I – New York

cent excess sales. As will be noted, the blocking out of these spaces will form rectangles with the greatest dimen-sion vertical instead of horizontal as in the group of rectangles X. This helps to differentiate the excess sales areas from those of the full quota.

The line of rectangles Z in each state's section is provided for recording the cumulative monthly percentages of actual sales as measured by the year's sales quota (assigned in Chart 1-A) and the open space immediately below line Z is provided to indicate any cumulative excess over and above the quota just as in the case of section Y for monthly excess of sales over quota. Thus, at any time, it may be seen from a glance at the upper or monthly group of X rectangles, whether or not the monthly sales have equalled or exceeded the quota, while the lower line of rectangles Z will show just as quickly the same information for the entire period of the year elapsed from the date of starting the chart.

Specifically, the five rectangles X at the top of the monthly section are filled out in proportion to the actual sales made during the month, in accordance with the following. Block out all five of these rectangles X, if the sales for the month exactly equal the sales quota. In the case of Alabama (Chart 2-A), with potential sales of 63,683, a yearly quota of 636, and a monthly quota of one-twelfth of that quantity, 53, at an average price of $100 per machine, the sales required to meet this quota would amount to $5,300 per month and $63,600 per year. It will be noted that the quota may thus be expressed in terms of money as well as machines since the one unit is translated into the other by the simple process of multiplication.

As the first or top rectangle of section X in the January column of the State of Alabama represents 20% of the monthly quota of 53 machines, the entire area of this first rectangle would be locked out if 11 machines were sold in January; four rectangles would be blocked out if 43 machines were sold; and all five of the rectangles X would be blocked out if 53 machines were sold.

Section Y in each monthly column is provided for recording the excess over 100% of the sales quota and is blocked out from left to right as far as is necessary. If 120% of the monthly quota is sold, section Y is blocked out as far as the first vertical line; if 140% is sold, section Y is filled in to the second vertical line; if 180%, to the fourth vertical line; and the entire section, if 200% is sold.

The space below section Z is provided for indicating sales in excess of the yearly quota.

While there are 12 rectangles across the chart in section Z, none of these rectangles refers to any particular month of the year. The whole 12 represent the full sales quota for the year and each individual rectangle represents 1/12th of the year's quota of sales or 8 1/3rd percent. For example, if 8 1/3% of the year's sales quota is sold during the 1st month (or the first two or three or more months) the first rectangle in Section Z is to be blocked out; if 50% of the year's sales quota is sold by July 31st, the first 6 blocks of Section Z are blocked out, thus indicating that for the first 7 months the sales proceeded at only 50% of the yearly sales quota rate. The blocking out of Section Z is continuous and unbroken and has reference only to recording the percentage of the year's quota and not the percentage of any month's quota.

In Chart 2-A, Alabama, for the month of January, four X rectangles are blocked out, indicating that actual sales reached only 80% of the sales quota. Section Z is therefore blocked out to the extent of 80% of the first division of the section. Alabama for the month of February shows 100% of Section X blocked out and one sub-division of Section Y, indicating actual sales of 20% in excess, or 120%, of the sales quota for February. For the two months, January and February, as 80% of the monthly quota was sold in January and 120% in February, the total sales for the two months are 200%, or exactly 100% per month, and Section Z is therefore blocked out to the extent of 2/12ths of the year's quota, which, in this case, blocks it out exactly to the end of the February subdivision.

APPENDIX B

ADVERTISING CONTROL

Chart 3-A was designed to follow in detail the quota for advertising in each state, by months and for the year. The first column indicates the states and the second column the advertising appropriation for each state, per month and per year. Each of the next twelve columns on the chart covers a month of the year; and the top group of rectangles X across each state section represents the quota for each month's advertising expense. Here is blocked out for each month, just as in Chart 2-A, that percentage of the total area of these rectangles which the actual advertising expenditure bears to the month's appropriation for advertising. Sections X, Y and Z are also blocked out with reference to the advertising quota and the actual expenditures, in the same manner as Chart 2-A is blocked out with reference to the sales quota and the actual sales made.

For Alabama, in the month of January, 5 X rectangles and 2½ Y rectangles are blocked out, indicating the expenditure of 150% of the monthly appropriation for that state. Section Z was therefore blocked out to the extent of the first rectangle and ½ of the second rectangle. For the month of February the advertising expenditures again exceeded the monthly appropriation by 50%. With expenditures of 150% in January and 150% in February, the combined expenditures for the two months were 50% in excess of the appropriation for those months.

Section Z is therefore blocked out completely in the January and February rectangles and the excess expenditures fall into the next rectangle, carrying the blocking

146

out through the March rectangle, and indicating that three
times 8 1/3% (the value of each Z rectangle) or 25% of
the year's full quota has been spent.

ADVERTISING QUOTA CONTROL CHART

TERRITORY	APPROPRIATION	YEAR 1925											
		JAN	FEB	MAR	APR	MAY	JUNE	JULY	AUG	SEPT	OCT	NOV	DEC
ALABAMA	PER MONTH—$265												
	PER YEAR — $3,180												
ARIZONA	PER MONTH—$ 65												
	PER YEAR — $ 785												
ARKANSAS	PER MONTH —$ 244												
	PER YEAR — $ 2925												
CALIFORNIA	PER MONTH—$ 2,840												
	PER YEAR — $ 34,085												
COLORADO	PER MONTH—$ 502												
	PER YEAR — $ 6,020												
CONNETICUT	PER MONTH—$ 607												
	PER YEAR — $ 7,280												
DELAWARE	PER MONTH—$ 47												
	PER YEAR — $ 560												
FLORIDA	PER MONTH—$ 340												
	PER YEAR — $ 4,070												
GEORGIA	PER MONTH—$ 408												
	PER YEAR—$4,900												
IDAHO	PER MONTH—$ 193												
	PER YEAR—$ 2315												

No. 3ᴀ   copyrighted · 1925 · BY W. A. SAVAGE · G. R. F. MONTOR

APPENDIX C

PRODUCTION CONTROL

In a manufacturing concern, the problem of maintaining a proper balance between the various departments is always vital. This balance is influenced by a great many conditions and necessarily must be continually under surveillance. The keeping of this balance is a question of management, with all that management involves; and the graphic means of showing the balanced or unbalanced condition between each department and the production as a whole is invaluable as an aid to management.

The elements which enter into this means of visualizing the production condition, are the productive capacity of the plant as a whole and the allotment to the respective departments of production quotas necessary to maintain the desired output.

For the concern used as an illustration it was determined that the maximum annual capacity was normally 75,000 machines, and the quotas and appropriations were made on this basis, as shown on Charts Nos. 1-A, 2-A, 3-A and 4-A. The "Production Control Chart," No. 4-A, represents the maximum production capacity, or 75,000 machines per year. The measure of each department's monthly production is shown by the number of horizontal rectangles filled-in under each month, and of its total production, by the length of the cumulative rectangle, Z.

The five horizontal rectangles, X, under each month represent 100%' of the monthly production quota shown in the column on the left. Should only 60% of the monthly

148

quota be accomplished, 3 of the 5 rectangles would be filled in; if 40%, 2 of the rectangles would be filled in. In any case, the open horizontal rectangles represent the unfinished portion of the quota. However, should the production for

PRODUCTION CONTROL CHART

— No. 4 A —

copyrighted - 1925 by W.A. Savage - B.R.I-NY

any month exceed the quota, say by 40%, the five horizontal rectangles representing 100% would be filled in and, in addition, 2 of the vertical rectangles, Y, immediately below, indicating 140% production for the month.

Similarily, for the cumulative production, if for the first month only 50% of the quota was attained, only half of the rectangle, Z, within the broken lines would be filled in. Likewise, if at the end of the 4th month only 75% of the quota for the first four months was fulfilled, the cumulative rectangle would be filled in for the first three months, indicating that production at the end of the 4th month was 25% behind the schedule, and that instead of completing 33 1/3% of the annual quota only 25% was completed.

The following is a departmental percentage schedule of production for the first six months.

	PARTS							Assembly		Complete
	1	2	3	4	5	6	7	1st	2nd	Machines
Jan.	20%	40%	100%	90%	100%	100%	90%	20%	90%	20%
Feb.	40	60	100	100	100	100	90	40	90	40
March	80	100	100	110	100	90	100	80	100	80
April	100	110	90	90	80	110	100	100	100	100
May	140	150	100	100	80	100	110	140	80	140
June	150	140	110	110	140	100	110	150	140	150

Because of lack of materials in January and February, departments 1 and 2 did not produce their monthly quota, resulting in a general tie-up in the 1st Assembly department and necessitating overtime work in the later months.

The effect of this situation may not seem apparent, but in reality it has brought about a condition that has reacted very unfavorably on both the 2nd Assembly department and the Completed Machine department. At the end of June it has left the 1st Assembly department with 70% of a month's supply of Parts 2, 3 and 4 because of the excess of production in these parts over Part 1 in the earlier months. Likewise the Completed Machines department is left with an excess of 70% of a month's quota of the 2nd Assembly department. It has, therefore, tied up capital that otherwise might have been working, and has necessitated overtime work with its resulting increase in costs.

This chart, showing a picture of production progress and its exact position in regard to production capacity, becomes a supporting factor to sound management. It furnishes an estimated or planned production against which can be recorded the actual production, thus facilitating a comparison of the planned and actual production and determining quickly the source of any variation from the schedule.

It places the executive in a position to determine when it is necessary to revise his schedules to relieve congestion or to meet conditions caused by lack of materials, absentees, or breakdowns of machinery, and where to apply pressure to secure an even flow of production.

In a sense the "Production Control Chart" forces a consideration of standardization. The determination of maximum production capacity is standardization work. Furthermore standardization work is sure to follow the introduction of a "Production Control Chart," because, in such a chart, the losses due to lack of standardization show so clearly. Indirectly, graphic production control leads to cost control for so long as a job or operation is up to or ahead of the schedule, costs are bound to be within the prescribed limits.

The principal functions of Chart No. 4-A are to turn the searchlight on deficiencies and failures in management, and to spot any tie-up in capital which may occur. When departmental production is continuous the effect of lack of control becomes evident at once. Under casual and haphazard management the output flows from department to department by fits and starts. The stream of material is dammed up in one department until the work becomes hurried and careless. The wrathful descent of the executive upon the head of the department only adds to the confusion of those who are unlucky enough to cross his path. Workmen rush wildly about making mistakes, material is spoiled, and men stand idle while the executive berates his subordinates.

Meanwhile, men in the preceding departments loaf because the floor and benches are piled high with work that cannot be passed on and men in the succeeding departments loaf because no work can be sent to them.

It is a sad fact that, in matters pertaining to production control, there is less definite knowledge of its possibilities than in any other phase of industrial activity. Where efficiency of production is concerned, our manufacturers, perhaps, are second to none, but the determination and control of the rate of production appears to present such difficulties that the task has been seriously neglected.

A

Accountability, line of....... 130
Accounting, charts in........ 1
Accounts receivable 23
Accumulation of surplus..... 38
Actual vs. budget estimates... 110
Accuracy of charts........14, 91
Accuracy of estimates........ 103
Adaptability of charts....... 82
Administration expenses 46
Administration in organization 130
Administrative control charts. 16
Advertising considerations ... 70
Advertising control 146
Allotment of customers 78
Analysis of balance sheet and
   income statement 16
Analysis of branch sales 74
Analysis of budget estimates . 99
Analysis of costs 81
Analysis of customers 72
Analysis of departmental sales 65
Analysis of income 52, 57
Analysis of material, labor and
   overhead 83
Analysis of profit and loss.... 57
Analysis of sales
         46, 49, 53, 55, 58, 65
Analysis of salesmen's reports 65
Analysis of sales territory ... 78
Analysis of selling plan 78
Analytical records 13
Annual return on capital stock
   investment 40
Assets, current.............. 20
Assets, fixed 35
Assets vs. liabilities.......... 18
Average costs 88

B

Bad debts 25
Balance sheet, analysis of.... 16
Bondholders interests 38
Bar chart, vertical, sales...... 141
Borrowed capital 38
Branch sales, analysis of..... 74
Budget estimate, analysis of.. 99
Budget estimate, check on.... 105
Budget estimate, form....102, 112
Burden of excess plant invest-
   ment 30

Business forecasting 14, 26
Business possibilities 68

C

Capital, turnover of 41
Cash 22
Cash balances 23
Cash discount 105, 111
Cash position 21
Cash vs. current liabilities.... 19
Charges, fixed 104
Charges to surplus 44
Charts, clarity of 14
Charts, comparative value of . 14
Charts, continuity of 13, 85
Charts, control value 6
Charts, educational value 8
Charts, simplicity of 7
Charts, speed of 7
Charts, time saving features.. 7
Charts, uses in comparisons .. 13
Charts, uses in expressing
   movements of finances..... 10
Charts, uses in World War ... 5
Charts, value in making deci-
   sions 6
Charts, value of continuity... 13
Check, on budget estimates... 105
Chronological charts 88
Clerical routine 117
Collection policy 23
Committee type of organization 134
Commodity sales 49, 76
Common uses of visualization. 2
Comparative importance of
   fluctuations 82
Competitive considerations .. 33
Compilation of costs........ 81
Conservatism, degree of...... 34
Consumption, stock 94
Content and purpose of ad-
   ministrative control charts . 16
Control, by means of visualiza-
   tion 2
Control, stores 93
Co-ordination of information 6, 14
Co-ordination of sales and pro-
   duction 111
Co-ordination routine methods. 117
Corporate requirements 104
Correlation of inventory and
   production 27, 111

Cost analysis 81
Cost fluctuations 82
Cost of sales 49
Cost per dollar of sales....... 44
Costs, average 88
Costs, chronological chart of.. 88
Costs, controlling factors of.. 85
Costs, labor 87, 92
Costs, material 87, 92
Costs, overhead 87, 92
Costs, per pound 89
Costs, proportionate value of 84, 90
Costs, total 85
Costs, unit 81
Costs, variation of 91
Costs vs. production.......84, 85
Current assets 18
Current liabilities 18
Customers, allotment of...... 78

D

Degree of accuracy of esti-
  mates 103
Degree of conservatism 34
Degree of earning power..... 40
Desirable limits fixed by charts
           28, 30, 33, 34
Detection of errors.......... 91
Detection value of charts.... 14
Development of sales territory 69
Discount, cash 105
Dividends, requirements 42
Dollar value of sales......... 44

E

Earning power, degree of 40
Earning power of plant invest-
  ment 30
Educational value of charts .. 8
Effective uses of graphic charts 3
Effort, salesmen's 69
Elements of cost........... 83
Emphasis produced by charts. 15
Equation, minimum sales re-
  quirement 107
Errors, detection of.......14, 91
Estimate (budget) vs. actual. 109
Estimates, preparation of.... 100
Excessive reserves 35
Expenses, fixed 92, 104
Expenses, variable 104

F

Factory order routine........ 128
Factory order, uses of........ 129
Financial movement of business 10
Finished goods turnover...... 26
Fixed assets 35
Fixed expenses 92, 104
Forecasting collections 25
Forecasting reserves 42
Function of graphics......... 1
Functional organization 138

G

Graphic analysis 12
Graphic chart, function of.... 1
Graphics and pictures....... 10
Graphics, common uses 2
Graphics, for supervision 7
Graphics, in industry 6
Graphics, in the World War.. 5
Graphics, original uses 3

I

Illustrations, newspaper uses. 8
Income and expense, analysis
  of 44, 110
Increase, rate of, measured by
  slope 35
Inter-relation of cost elements 91
Inventory and production 111
Inventory, turnover 26
Investment, stockholders 42
Influencing salesmen 65
Introduction of new ideas.... 68

J

Jobbing or wholesale marketing costs 92

L

Labor costs, analysis of....87, 92
Labor routine 123
Liabilities, current 18
Liabilities, fixed 38
Limits of desirability fixed by
  charts 28, 30, 33, 34
Line and staff type of organi-
  zation 137

Line type of organization.... 135
Lines of responsibility....... 130

M

Manufacturing costs 92
Management, functions 131
Material expenses 91
Material, ordering 121
Material routine 121
Materials and supplies, turn-
over 26
Maximum expenses 104
Measuring percentage of vari-
ation 35
Memory aided by charts...... 3
Military type of organization. 135
Minimum sales requirement .. 104
Money invested in inventory .. 26
Money invested in property and
plant 30

N

Necessity for budget......... 99
Net return on invested capital 40
New ideas, introduction of... 68
Notes and loans receivable.... 25
Notes payable vs. cash....... 23

O

Office procedure 117
Order routine, factory 128
Ordering material 121
Orderly arrangement of facts
10, 13
Organization charts 130
Organization, committee type . 137
Organization, functional sub-
divisions 138
Organization, functional type . 130
Organization, line or military
type 135
Organization, line and staff
type 137
Overbuying, to prevent...... 96
Overhead costs, analysis of... 87
Outside adviser 119

P

Perpetual inventory, charts for 93

Physical activity of a business 10
Planning of sales effort...... 70
Policy, collection 23
Policy formation 12
Position, cash 21
Preparation of estimates..... 100
Procedure, routine 117
Production and inventory . 27, 113
Production control 148
Production control charts 112
Production, in pounds........ 86
Production vs. sales 27, 113
Profit and loss, analysis of... 57
Profits 52
Progress chart, advertising... 147
Progress chart, production.... 149
Progress chart, sales........ 143
Property and plant investment 30
Proportionate value of costs.. 91
Psychology of graphic charts. 10

R

Range between sales and profit 52
Ratio charts 35
Raw materials and supplies,
turnover 26
Reference value of charts.... 13
Relations shown by adminis-
trative control charts...... 17
Requirements, corporate 104
Requirements, sales 104
Requirements, sinking fund .. 104
Reserves 34
Responsibility, lines of....... 130
Retrospective record 63
Risk of borrowed capital..... 40
Routine, charts 117
Routine, factory order 128
Routine, labor 123
Routine, material 123
Routine methods, co-ordination
of 117
Routine procedure 117

S

Sales 65
Sales, actual vs. estimated.... 109
Sales and profits 52
Sales, commodity 49, 76
Sales control 139
Sales, departmental 65

Sales quotas 139
Sales requirements, minimum . 104
Sales vs. costs 85
Sales vs. production 27, 113
Salesmen, interpretation to... 65
Salesmen's effort, analysis of. 71
Salesmen's records, charts of . 65
Seasonal variations 49
Selling an idea by charts..... 68
Selling plan, analysis of..... 78
Service of graphic charts..... 1
Semi-logarithmic charts 35
Simplicity of charts......... 7
Speed of charts............. 7
Stabilization of profits 15
Staff and line type of organi-
    zation 137
Stock consumption 93
Stock records 93
Stock requirements 97
Stockholders interests 42
Stores control 93
Summary sheet 59
Supply (inventory) 26
Surplus accumulation 44
Surplus charges 44
Surplus, deductions from 44

T

Territory, analysis 74
Territory, development 78
Total costs of production..... 85
Turnover of accounts receiv-
    able 23
Turnover of capital 41
Turnover of finished goods in-
    ventory 26
Turnover of property and plant
    investment 30

Turnover of raw materials and
    supplies inventory 26
Turnover of total inventory .. 26

U

Uncollectable accounts 25
Unit costs 81
Uses of budget control charts. 99
Uses of graphic charts in com-
    parisons 13
Uses of graphic charts in World
    War 5

V

Value of charts, in making de-
    cisions 6
Value of continuity of charts.. 13
Value of expert counsel 119
Variable expenses 104
Variation of costs........... 91
Visualization in the World
    War 5
Volume of inventory, produc-
    tion and sales............ 113
Volume of production.....27, 113
Volume of sales 65

W

Wall charts 60
Wholesale marketing costs.... 92
Working capital ratio........ 18

Y

Yearly return on capital stock
    investment 40

SAMPLE SETS

There are now nearly 200 different kinds of Codex Data Paper (including thin and heavy sheets) and, much as we should like to, it is not practicable to send free samples of all of these to the many who ask for them. We have, therefore, adopted the plan of making up Sample Sets which include a full-sized sheet of every ruling. To avoid duplicates and bulkiness most of the rulings in the Sample Sets are on thin paper but nearly all of them may be had on heavy paper also, if preferred. These sets are sold at cost with no allowance for "on approval" orders or collection charges, etc. Therefore, kindly send remittance with order. Or, if preferred, we will gladly send C. O. D.

Complete Set of Sample Sheets (about 100 sheets) $2.00, postpaid.

SHEETS DESIGNED FOR THE ECONOMIC CONSTRUCTION OF GRAPHIC CHARTS

SHEETS DIVIDED INTO VARIOUS PERIODS OF TIME

The following are specially designed for business statistics. The base lines are divided to cover specific periods of time—days, weeks, months, years, etc. For example, One Year by Months indicates that the sheet covers a total period of one year which is subdivided into months. See Fig. 5. On most of the sheets the numbers of the days, names of the months, etc., are printed. Most of these sheets may be had with plain ruling or with ratio ruling, as desired, Figs. 5 and 6.

PLAIN RULING

Size of Sheets, ins.	8½x11		11x16½	
Kind of Paper	Thin	Heavy	Thin	Heavy
Prices, as Shown on Page 1.				
One Day by Hours	3176	3276	—	—
One Week by Hours	—	—	4159	—
One Month by Days	3139	3239	—	—
Six Months by Days	—	—	4159	—
*One Year by Days (Calendar Year)	3117	3217	4117	4217
*One Year by Days (Calendar Year)	—	—	4186	4286
One Year by Days (Any Fiscal Year)	—	—	4119	4219
One Yr. by Working Days (52 Main Divisions of 6 Days Each)	—	—	4195	4295
One Year by Weeks	3137	3237	—	—
One Year by Months (Months Short Way of Paper)	3141	3241	—	—
One Year by Months (Months Long Way of Paper)	3148	3248	—	—
Two Years by Mos.	3150	3250	—	—
Three Years by Mos.	3166	3266	—	—
Five Years by Mos.	3122	3222	—	—
Ten Years by Mos.	—	—	4156	4256
Twenty Years by Mos	—	—	4171	4271
Three Yrs by Mos. / Sixteen Yrs. by Yrs.	same sheet		4177	4277

** On Nos. 4117 and 4217 the vertical scale is divided into 10 divisions per unit, on Nos 4186 and 4286 into 8 divisions per unit. The latter are used a great deal for Stock and Bond prices, etc.*

RATIO RULING

Size of Sheets, ins.	8½x11		11x16½	
Kind of Paper	Thin	Heavy	Thin	Heavy
Prices, as Shown on Page 1				
One Mo. by Days (3 cycles)	3140	3240	—	—
One Yr by Days (3 cycles) (Calendar Year)	—	—	4118	4218
One Yr by Days (3 cycles) (Any Fiscal Year)	—	—	4120	4220
One Yr. by Wks. (3 cycles)	3138	3238	—	—
One Yr. by Mos. (3 cycles) (Months Short Way of Paper)	3142	3242	—	—
One Yr by Mos. (2 cycles) (Months Long Way of Paper)	3149	3249	—	—
Two Yrs by Mos. (2 cycles)	3151	3251	—	—
Three Yrs by Mos (2 cy's)	3167	3267	—	—
Five Yrs. by Mos (3 cycles)	3155	3255	—	—
Ten Yrs. by Mos (3 cycles)	—	—	4157	4257
Twenty Yrs. by Mos. (3 cycles)	—	—	4172	4272
Three Yrs by Mos. / Sixteen Yrs. by Yrs	same sheet		4178	4278

WIDE MARGIN CHART SHEETS

These sheets have a ruled charting section 4 by 6⅔ ins. in one corner, leaving a clear space of 4¼ ins. at the left and top for putting data on same sheet with chart. Fig 10. This style of chart sheet is frequently used for the so-called Z charts advocated by Arthur R. Burnet.

Size of Sheet, ins.	8½x11
Kind of Paper	Thin
Prices, as Shown on Page 1.	
One Year by Weeks	3147
One Year by Months	3146

CROSS-SECTION CHART SHEETS.

The following have plain arithmetic ruling and are most generally know as "cross-section" or "quadrille ruled" papers. Some have the same number of subdivisions per inch both ways of the sheet, others are divided into a different number of divisions per unit one way from what they are the other. Figs. 1 and 2 on page 4 illustrate the two types. The following have heavier lines at the main division points with lighter lines for the subdivisions.

Size of Sheet, ins.	4¼x7¼	8½x11		11x16½	
Kind of Paper	Thin	Thin	Heavy	Thin	Heavy
Prices, as Shown on Page 1.					
4 by 4 Div. per Inch	211	311	—	—	—
5 by 5 " " "	212	312	—	—	—
6 by 6 " " "	213	313	—	—	—
8 by 8 " " "	214	314	—	414	—
10 by 10 " " "	215	315	325	415	425
12 by 12 " " "	216	316	—	—	—
16 by 16 " " "	217	317	—	—	—
20 by 20 " " " (½ inch margins)	218	318	328	418	428
20 by 20 " " " (1 inch margins)	—	3110	3210	—	—
Millimeters (½ inch margins)	219	319-A	—	—	—
Millimeters (1 inch margins)	—	319	329	419	429
6 by 8 Div. per Unit	—	3165	3265	—	—
12 by 10 " " "	—	3164	3264	—	—
4 by 10 " " " / 12 by 10 same sheet	—	3121	3221	—	—
12 by 20 Div. per Unit	2114	3114	3214	4114	4214

On the following all of the lines are of uniform heaviness, there being no heavier lines at the main division points, Figs. 3 and 4.

Size of Sheet, ins.	8½x11	
Kind of Paper	Thin	Heavy
Prices, as Shown on Page 1.		
10 by 10 Div. per Inch	3187	3287
20 by 20 " " "	3188	3288
2 by 2⅔ " " "	3184	3284

POLYPURPOSE SHEETS

These sheets are so-called because the heaviness of the vertical ruling is uniform and the lines may be so accented as to divide the sheets into any desired periods of time. Figs. 7 and 8 are typical.

PLAIN RULING

Size of Sheet, ins.	8½x11		11x16½	
Kind of Paper	Thin	Heavy	Thin	Heavy
Prices, as Shown on Page 1.				
12 by 20 Div. per Inch	3111	3211	4111	4211

RATIO RULING

Size of Sheets, ins.	8½x11		11x16½	
Kind of Paper	Thin	Heavy	Thin	Heavy
Prices, as Shown on Page 1.				
12 Div. per In. by 1 9" Cycle	3134	3234	4134	4234
12 Div. per In. by 2 4½" Cyc's	3135	3235	4135	4235
12 Div per In. by 3 3" "	3112	3212	—	—
12 Div. per In. by 4 2¼" "	3174	3274	—	—
12 Div. per In. by 5 1⅘" "	3175	3275	—	—
6 Div. per In. by 5 3" "	—	—	4113	4213
2 Div. per In. by 2 4½" "	3185	3285	—	—

OTHER RATIO RULINGS

The following have plain ruling, 20 divisions per inch, horizontally, every half-inch division line being accented and every inch line more heavily accented, and have ratio ruling vertically.

Size of Sheet, ins.	8½x11		11x16½	
Kind of Paper	Thin	Heavy	Thin	Heavy
Prices, as Shown on Page 1.				
20 Div. per In. by 2 3¾" Cycles	3115	3215	—	—
20 Div. per In. by 3 3" Cycles	—	—	4115	4215

Note: The figures (Fig. 1, Fig. 2, etc.) mentioned in the above descriptions of the chart sheets refer to illustrations in our price list. Upon request we will be very glad to send you a copy of this list.

CODEX BOOK CO., Inc. **461 EIGHTH AVE., NEW YORK**

FLEXIBLE SCALE SHEETS

These sheets embody an advanced idea in graphic chart making. They have no horizontal cross-lines, only vertical ones to indicate the time intervals. The scale, either plain or ratio, is constructed by drawing in as many or as few horizontal lines as desired with the aid of the Codex Scale Divider. The intermediate points between these main scale lines are plotted with the Scale Divider, so designed that it fits any scale range desired. Fig. 9.

Size of Sheet, ins.	—8½x11—		11x16½
Kind of Paper	Thin	Heavy	Heavy
Prices, as Shown on Page 1.			
One Month by Days		32100	—
One Year by Months		32103	—
Three Years by Months			42106
Polypurpose			42110
(72 uniform vertical lines)			
Scale Divider	3160		—

"TWO-IN-ONE" CHART SHEETS

Upon these sheets are two chart panels of equal size abreast of each other—one with plain ruling, the other with ratio ruling.

The purpose is to show, side by side, a chart which gives a correct picture of the numerical variations and a chart which gives in their true proportions a picture of the percentage variations, for any set of data. In short, upon one and the same sheet you get "the whole story."

	Plain and Ratio Ruling
Size of Sheet, ins.	—8½x11—
Kind of Paper	Thin Heavy
Prices, as Shown on Page 1.	
One Year by Months	3169 3269

CIRCULAR PERCENTAGE CHART SHEET

This sheet has three circles—one 6 ins., and two 2 ins., in diameter. The circumference of each is divided into 100 equal parts. These are for making the so-called "Pie Chart." Fig. 11.

Size of Sheet, ins.	—8½x11—	
Kind of Paper	Thin	Heavy
Prices, as Shown on Page 1		
Circular Percentage Chart	3116	3216

OUTLINE MAP OF UNITED STATES

On this map are shown the outlines of the states and no printing except the names of the states. Very useful for mapping out salesmen's routes; indicating population densities vs. orders, sales, etc. Fig. 13.

Size of Sheet, ins.	—8½x11—	
Kind of Paper	Thin	Heavy
Prices, as Shown on Page 1.		
U. S Outline Map	3133	3233

LOOSE LEAF BINDERS

For holding and filing chart sheets there is no device more satisfactory than the Loose-Leaf Ring Binder as it keeps the sheets in order and permits single sheets to be taken out or inserted without removing, or disturbing the order of, the rest of the sheets. We recommend binders with stiff canvas covers as they are rigid when filed on edge. See Fig 23.

Prices. Ring Binders, 3 1-inch rings 4¼ inches apart, to hold

8½x11 inch sheets	$1 30
11x16½ " "	2.75

BOOKS THAT CLEARLY EXPLAIN ALL ABOUT GRAPHIC CHARTS

GRAPHIC CHARTS IN BUSINESS

By Allan C. Haskell with an Introductory Chapter by Richard T. Dana. This book is for the business man. It does not go into mathematical theory but explains clearly and simply how to make and use charts for the analysis and graphic presentation of business statistics.

So far as we know it contains a more complete and simple explanation of the ratio chart than any other book on the market. This is important, for the ratio chart is the most useful to the business man. And for this reason—that most business men are concerned more with *relative* than with actual quantities when comparing their financial and operating facts, and the ratio chart is the only type which gives a correct picture of *percentage* variations and at the same time shows the actual values of the quantities compared.

The first half describes the various types of charts—bar charts, line charts, on both plain and ratio paper, circular percentage charts, organization charts, etc The last half explains and illustrates which of these types may be used to the best advantage for showing important facts and relationships in the accounting, advertising, collection, cost, credit, personnel, purchasing, sales, etc, departments There are over 200 illustrations in the book which aid very materially in making the various points clear.

Price $4 00, net, postpaid.

HOW TO MAKE AND USE GRAPHIC CHARTS

By Allan C Haskell with an Introductory Chapter by Richard T Dana. This book describes the application of graphic charts both to analysis and computation Due to the inclusion of the latter it is somewhat more technical than "Graphic Charts in Business," but for engineers and those interested in mathematical computation this volume contains much of value not taken up in the smaller book

In the first part of the book the following kinds of charts are explained Rectilinear, logarithmic, semi-logarithmic, polar, isometric, trilinear, alignment and organization. The rest of the book shows how these various types may be utilized to the best advantage in cost analysis, scheduling and progress, operating characteristics, results of tests and experiments; trends and tendencies, arithmetical and geometrical computation, designing and estimating, and various miscellaneous uses.

Price $6 00, net, postpaid.

SPECIAL SET PRICE

There is very little duplicated in the two books and taken together they pretty well cover the entire subject of graphic analysis. For this reason it is frequently desired to have both books in a set, and when purchased together in this way there is a saving of $1 00, the Special Set price being $9.00, postpaid.

BOOKS SENT ON APPROVAL

We are always glad to send our books on 10 days' approval to anyone who will furnish a satisfactory reference. There is no obligation whatever. Just send in a request on one of our return cards or on your business letterhead.

WHAT OTHERS THINK OF OUR BOOKS

The following are abstracts from a few of the letters we have received. To the majority of the writers the books had been sent on approval:

"It did not take me five minutes to decide that I would keep the copy of Haskell's Graphic Charts just received 'on suspicion' and I am enclosing my check herewith"

"This is a formal order for your book on graphic charts. The book was received on 10 days' trial and we like it so much that we had an order issued for same."

"The chapter on Organization and Management alone is worth the price of the book. The use of charts as applied to business efficiency is in its infancy but every business man should inform himself thoroughly relative to its application to his business."

"Please find enclosed my check in payment for one copy of How To Make and Use Graphic Charts which was received on approval. I have long felt want and presents data on charting which I have never before been able to find in print."

"How To Make and Use Graphic Charts is exactly what I have been looking for and every business man, engineer and student should have a copy."

"Upon an examination of Haskell's book on charts I desire to say in comment that I consider it the best brief treatise on the subject extant."

"Received Haskell's work on Graphic Charts and am more than pleased with it."

CONCRETE COMPUTATION CHARTS

This is a book consisting mostly of charts with an explanation of the methods of procedure, with very detailed examples for making all the computations necessary in concrete work. By the use of this book all the figuring on a plain and reinforced concrete job can be done in the easiest and simplest way and without mathematical work on the part of the computer The charts combine the information contained in a standard concrete handbook with the computing functions of a slide rule.

Bound in Flexible Keratol, $6 00, postpaid.

FITTING CALCULATOR

An effective labor-saving device for computing loss of power in electrical conductors. Consists of 3 circular slide rules, by the setting of which, with necessary tables of constants, the solutions are obtained.

Bound in Keratol, $10.00, postpaid.

We shall be very glad to send either the Concrete Computation Charts or the Fitting Calculator on 10 days' approval upon request.

CODEX BOOK CO., Inc.   461 EIGHTH AVE., NEW YORK